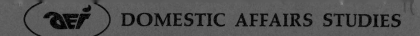

DOMESTIC AFFAIRS STUDIES

MATCHING NEEDS AND RESOURCES

Reforming the Federal Budget

Murray L. Weidenbaum
Dan Larkins
Philip N. Marcus

MATCHING NEEDS AND RESOURCES

MATCHING NEEDS AND RESOURCES:
Reforming the Federal Budget

Murray L. Weidenbaum
Dan Larkins
Philip N. Marcus

American Enterprise Institute for Public Policy Research
Washington, D. C.

ISBN 0-8447-3098-x

Domestic Affairs Study 11, March 1973

Library of Congress Catalog Card No. L.C. 73-79382

Printed in the United States of America

CONTENTS

All years are fiscal years unless otherwise noted. All data for the text and tables are taken from *Budget of the United States Government, Fiscal Year 1974* or *Special Analyses,* unless otherwise noted.

PREFACE

This report analyzes the key policy issues in President Nixon's proposed federal budget for fiscal 1974. After examining the realism and appropriateness of the revenue and expenditure estimates themselves, the report then deals with' the questions of tax reform and budget reform.

Chapters 1, 2, and 3 are primarily the work of the senior author, Murray L. Weidenbaum, Edward Mallinckrodt distinguished university professor at Washington University in St. Louis and adjunct scholar at the American Enterprise Institute for Public Policy Research. Dr. Weidenbaum served as assistant secretary of the Treasury for economic policy during 1969-71 and as a fiscal economist with the Bureau of the Budget from 1949 to 1957.

Chapter 4, and other materials in this report as well, were prepared by Dan Larkins, economist on the research staff of the American Enterprise Institute.

Chapters 5 and 6 were the primary responsibility of Philip N. Marcus, a research associate in political science at the American Enterprise Institute.

1
INTRODUCTION
AND SUMMARY

This analysis and review of the federal budget for the fiscal year 1974 confirms the impression conveyed in last year's study [1]—namely, that there is little if any leeway in the public fisc today for financing ambitious new undertakings with existing tax resources. Yet pressure for expensive new programs—national health insurance, development of new energy sources and Vietnam reconstruction—continues. Simultaneously, there is growing demand for action on the alleged inequities of the revenue side of the budget.

The bulk of this study is devoted to presenting practical alternatives for public discussion of these issues, specifically of matters dealing with budget reform and tax reform. An analysis of the fiscal policy proposed in the budget, however, is a necessary starting point.

Fiscal Policy

The basic thrust of the proposed 1974 budget accords with the current needs of the American economy, both domestic and international. Specifically, the budget's move in the direction of fiscal restraint before the full-employment point is reached should help to reduce the threat of rising inflation in the year ahead and to sustain the solid economic advance now underway. Reasonable men and women may differ about the specific program priorities in the budget (as shown in Chapter 2, there is virtual stability in the shares of the budget to be devoted to the major functional areas). But the proposed movements in the fiscal aggregates—total revenues, total outlays, and the resultant surplus or

---

[1] Murray L. Weidenbaum and Dan Larkins, *The Federal Budget for 1973* (Washington: American Enterprise Institute for Public Policy Research, 1972).

deficit—are receiving widespread support. The need for greater fiscal restraint has been underscored recently by the upward revisions of economic forecasts for calendar year 1973. The economic boom continues to pick up steam.

As government revenues rise with the economic expansion, the deficit in the unified budget is expected to peak in this fiscal year, 1973, and to decline sharply in the fiscal year beginning July 1, 1973. In the full-employment budget (wherein budget estimates are prepared on the arbitrary assumption that the unemployment rate is 4 percent), the modest $4 billion deficit of fiscal 1972 becomes a $2 billion deficit this fiscal year, and approximate balance is looked for in fiscal 1974. Given the rising concern at home and abroad over the renewal of inflationary pressures in the United States, it is hard to make a case for a more stimulative fiscal policy (see Chapter 4 for an analysis of the effect of wage-price controls). And the concern that the new budget goes too far in the direction of restraint does not appear to be warranted. A $4 billion shift in the full-employment budget over a 24-month period is actually quite modest.

For those who are aware of the technical limitations of preparing the unified budget on a full-employment basis, we can refer to full-employment estimates based on the national income accounts basis.[2] Those data show a more mixed pattern, a movement from restraint to ease this year and shift back to restraint in fiscal 1974. The shift from a $9.4 billion full-employment deficit in fiscal 1973 to a $1.6 billion deficit in fiscal 1974 is also a rather modest, but desirable move.

A smaller federal deficit in 1974 should ease the pressures on financial markets and lighten the heavy load now borne by the Federal Reserve System. Also, by curtailing the government's need for additional borrowing it will yield welcome reduction in the upward pressure on interest rates.

In discussing any new budget, a word is usually in order on the realism of the budget estimates, and the 1974 budget is no exception. On the revenue side, the budget report surprisingly uses the same revenue projections for fiscal 1973 that were used in the revisions issued in the fall of 1972. Given the economy's strong performance in the fourth quarter of 1972 and given the upward revision of the GNP estimates for calendar 1973, an increase of several billion dollars in federal revenue should occur. It thus appears that the administration is "reserving" a modest amount of additional revenues in fiscal

---

[2] Federal Reserve Bank of St. Louis, *Federal Budget Trends*, period ending: 4th quarter, 1972, February 14, 1973.

year 1973 as an offset against the possibility it will not achieve all of the expenditure cuts planned for the current fiscal year. The 1974 revenue figures seem to be quite reasonable.

On the expenditure side, the Nixon administration's new hard look at government spending programs has received a sympathetic response from liberal as well as conservative quarters, even though disagreements about spending priorities persist. Typifying the general reaction, Richard Rovere has commented: "No one can deny that the federal government is a bloated beast, most of whose departments could function more effectively with far fewer people on the payroll, or that many programs have outlived their usefulness completely." [3] Indeed, the budget document proposes generous support for most domestic social welfare programs. In many cases, of course, this is the result of binding statutory legislation, the debate on the "impoundment power" notwithstanding. Nevertheless, despite the rhetoric on both sides, it is important to note that the 1974 budget would continue to provide many tens of billions of dollars for America's poor and that the administration's own forecasts for 1975 show a continuation of this trend.

The fact of the matter is that, for 1973, 1974 and 1975 (preliminary), the projected rise in domestic spending is many times greater than that in military spending. Domestic outlays are to increase by an impressive $34.0 billion during 1973 and 1974, and most of the increase is in social security, medicare, and related types of income-maintenance and income-transfer programs. In striking contrast, defense outlays are estimated to rise by a total of $2.8 billion from fiscal 1972 to 1974 (with a decline of $1.9 billion projected from 1972 to 1973 due to the cease-fire in Vietnam).

Also on the spending side, one concern is the omission of allowances for new initiatives, including those of the administration itself. The explanation usually offered by the administration—that any spending increases beyond those already budgeted will be financed by cuts in other programs—is difficult to count on. This is especially true of the anticipated outlays for rebuilding Vietnam. The budget also omits the major domestic initiatives which last year's presidential messages indicated were being developed for "relieving the burden of property taxes and providing fair and adequate financing for our children's education."

Moreover, there is a trace of excessive enthusiasm in the numerous expenditure "savings" listed in the budget. Much of the projected

---

[3] Richard H. Rovere, "Letter From Washington," *The New Yorker*, February 17, 1973, p. 89.

large cutback in farm subsidies, for example, should result merely from exogenous factors such as rising aggregate demand. Thankfully, no credit was claimed for a similar "cutback" in unemployment insurance payments which will result from the expected decline in unemployment. Also, to include on the list of executive reductions the savings to result from the congressionally enacted ceiling on social service grants seems to be stretching the point.

The proposed expenditure savings also reflect considerable optimism concerning the administration's ability to bring about quick and substantial improvements in the efficiency of government operations. The budget contains numerous references to expenditure reductions to be realized from the following vague methods: "Tighten operations . . . ," "Reduce . . . working capital requirements," "Achieve economies . . . ," "Increase efficiency . . . ," "Strengthen . . . cost controls," "Strengthen . . . management," "Provide more efficient . . . service," "Require more effective supply practices."

Yet possible exaggeration about reductions should not obscure the basic features of the new budget. The estimates for 1974 outlays, revenues and hence the deficit are quite reasonable. Whether or not a precise balance is achieved in the "full-employment budget" in the coming year, it does seem clear that the administration's efforts will result in a lower level of spending and a smaller deficit in the actual budget than would have been the case without those efforts. *All in all, the 1974 budget proposes a fiscal policy that seems well designed to meet the needs of the economy in the year ahead.*

Tax Reform

Last fall's often frenzied, uninformed debate on tax reform has subsided, but widespread dissatisfaction with the alleged inequities of the tax system is still evident. This study does not attempt the overly ambitious task of addressing the entire federal tax structure. Rather, it focuses on a single proposal (see Chapter 3) in the hope that it will further responsible tax reform. Specifically, it sets forth an alternative in the important but limited area of allowable personal expenses—that is, the current method of deducting certain taxes, interest payments, charitable donations, health expenses, and other items from gross taxable income. Under current law, the federal government in effect subsidizes 70 percent of the charitable donations and other designated outlays of individuals and families in the highest tax bracket, 14 percent of the deductible outlays of those in the lowest bracket, and somewhere in between for all others (except for taxpayers using the standard deduction, whose tax liability is not affected at all by the allowable expenses they actually incur).

The suggestion outlined here—to substitute tax credits for tax deductions—is designed to eliminate what appears to be an inequity in the status quo while maintaining the valuable supports for private and local institutions provided by the present arrangements. In its essence, the tax credit mechanism substitutes a neutral or progressive device for a regressive provision in the Internal Revenue Code. Yet, it recognizes the importance of fostering nonfederal solutions to national problems. Under a credit, every taxpayer, regardless of the size of his or her income, would qualify for the same tax benefit per dollar of allowable expense. For example, a 50 percent credit would permit every taxpayer giving $200 to charity to have his or her tax bill reduced by the same amount, $100.

Budget Reform

The ordering of national priorities contained in the 1974 budget is, of course, highly debatable. Yet, one fundamental point emerges. Even after a determined and undoubtedly difficult effort to curtail government programs, federal outlays for 1974 are still expected to rise by $19 billion over 1973 or by almost 8 percent. A total of $17 billion in attempted reductions was necessary merely to hold projected 1974 federal outlays within 21 percent of a rapidly growing gross national product. The need for more effective regular controls over federal programs and expenditures is increasingly clear.

How to improve the procedures through which the Congress makes its decisions on the budget is the subject of Part Two of this study. In the half century that has elapsed since the passage of the historic Budget and Accounting Act of 1921, numerous valuable improvements have been made in the manner in which the executive branch prepares the budget and justifies proposed undertakings—program budgeting, cost/effectiveness analysis, the unified budget, et cetera. But, the equally vital task of congressional review, modification, and approval of executive budget proposals still conforms in the main to the practices of what is surely a bygone age. The task at hand has been described in incisive language in a recent editorial:

> . . . Congress can either contribute greatly toward a constructive and fiscally sane budget, or it can muff the job. Before it can make a positive contribution, however, it must straighten out its own absurd and self-defeating budgetary and revenue procedures. The present nonsystem parcels out

7

the budget in so many directions that the overall budget picture is lost sight of and, with it, any real control.[4]

The Congress of course is not oblivious to its own shortcomings. Last year the Senate Finance Committee, in its report on the proposed expenditure ceiling, lamented that "in a period of strong, competing concepts of program priorities, all are accepted rather than choices among them being made."

A review of the historical development of the congressional budget process (see Chapter 5) shows that the present procedures have not always been with us, that change is possible and does occur. The Congress repeatedly has revised the manner in which it organizes for and takes action on budgetary matters. In a sense, there has been an ebb and flow from centralized to fragmentized decision making and back again. We may have reached a point where the tide of congressional power is about to flow once again.

This study offers no single, simple panacea. Rather, it recommends a package of changes (see Chapter 6) which in total would help to modernize the congressional budget process and thus increase the possibilities of more effective legislative action on financial matters. The major proposals are summarized here:

1. *Consolidate and simplify the budget.* It is unreasonable to expect the Congress to make rational choices among the many hundreds of programs, bureaus, agencies, and activities which it must review each year during the budget process. The use of a government-wide program budget—as outlined in last year's report [5]—would help to focus attention on major choices and the changing priorities that would result.

Above and beyond that, the basic nature of federal undertakings must be streamlined. Revenue sharing, both general and special, points the way to achieving national objectives with less federal overhead. The federal government is not suited for the role of "doer" or administrative manager of the entire vast array of undertakings that it finances in our society. Its great advantage is, rather, its ability to serve as a policy formulator, financier, and overseer over the public sector of the American economy. As shown in Chapter 3, the federal government can use the tax system to provide important assistance to other segments of the society without taking on the responsibility for running their activities—even when such activities promote a broad national interest.

---

[4] "Congress Must Contribute to Debate," *Christian Science Monitor*, January 31, 1973.

[5] Weidenbaum and Larkins, *The Federal Budget for 1973*, Chapter 4.

2. *Reorganize the appropriations committees.* It would be a great advantage if the subcommittee structure of the appropriations committees were reorganized to conform more closely to program lines. The prospect of an effective, coordinated review by Congress is undermined by a subcommittee structure patterned after department and agency lines that have been, or are in the process of being, abandoned. More basic, perhaps, is the need to strengthen the role of the House Appropriations Committee vis-à-vis its individual subcommittees. At the present time, the parent committee often resembles a loose confederation of autonomous individual components. If the various suggestions for strengthening the overall power of the committee were adopted, it would become even more important to make the subcommittees more responsive to the will and broader outlook of the full committee and thus of the Congress itself.

3. *Revise the congressional calendar.* The Congress cannot—and should not be expected to—complete work on the whole gamut of budget issues, general and specific, in the short period from February to June. It is not surprising, under the circumstances, that many appropriations bills are not passed until well after the new fiscal year begins.

The basic solution, of course, is to require that either the budget be submitted earlier or the fiscal year started later. In the absence of this change, the Congress should alter its own budget calendar. Hence, prior to the President's submission of the budget document, the committees should turn their attention to the basic economic, fiscal, and program policies that underlie the item-by-item decisions that are to come. There is a parallel in the executive branch: Office of Management and Budget (OMB) examiners often use lulls in the budget preparation process for detailed examinations and evaluations of specific programs that cannot be performed in the rush of the budget season.

4. *Enhance the role of the Economic Report of the President.* At the present time, the President's economic report tends to be submerged by his budget message and does not serve the central purposes for which it was intended. But if the report were submitted in early fall instead of January, then the Congress—prior to receiving the budget—would have a vehicle for exploring some of the basic issues it would have to address in the next session. Rather than being an after-the-fact rationalization of budgetary recommendations and decisions, the economic report could serve as a means of setting out some common intellectual ground for the program debates that would follow.

5. *Limit annual authorizations.* Many programs each year go through a double-barrelled process requiring, first, an authorization stating an amount to be appropriated and, second, the actual appropriation of funds. The advantages of annual authorizations—that is, better information, participation, and focus—recommend the practice despite the delays, duplication and inefficiency that may be its side-effects. A modification of present practices is needed.

Limited use of annual authorization is suggested here. Authorization should be completed before hearings on the actual budget begin. In addition, the authorizing committees should not prescribe dollar floors or ceilings for the programs whose authorization or reauthorization they are recommending. Setting the precise financial magnitudes of government programs should be the province of the appropriations committees.

6. *Use a special bill for appropriations increases to control spending.* The piecemeal approach to appropriations followed by congressional committees fails to control overall expenditures. Rather than again attempt the use of a spending ceiling or an omnibus appropriations bill to correct the fragmentation of budget authority,[6] a new approach should be tried: Congress should use a special appropriations bill for annual changes in total budget authority in order to apply a spending ceiling.

A spending target, or mandatory ceiling, would be established by congressional resolution. Marginal changes in total spending would be contained in a special appropriations bill sponsored by the chairmen of the appropriations committees. Each appropriations subcommittee would be limited to the amounts appropriated in the previous year for those activities under its jurisdiction, adjusted by a standard inflation factor.

Reallocation of funding by each subcommittee could be made freely within the ceilings established for each subcommittee. However, incremental changes in new budget authority from last year's level would be combined into one special bill. A new single bill would coordinate the use of numerous appropriations bills with a spending ceiling, reassembling program spending into a coordinated whole.

7. *Reduce backdoor financing.* At the present time, many federal programs escape the appropriations process entirely. A variety of transparent subterfuges are used to avoid formal appropriations.

---

[6] See U.S. Congress, Joint Study Committee on Budget Control, *Improving Congressional Control Over Budgetary Outlay and Receipt Totals* (Washington: U.S. Government Printing Office, 1973).

One is to provide financing for the program in the same bill that authorizes it. This frequently has been done in such areas as housing and agriculture. Another is the "authorization to spend public debt receipts." These authorizations require the Treasury to make disbursements in the same fashion as appropriations. The key difference, of course, is that the authority is not contained in an appropriations bill. The purpose of backdoor financing is obvious: the programs involved do not have to be justified to the appropriations committees but only to what often are the more sympathetic subject matter committees.

Backdoor financing makes it difficult for Congress to determine spending priorities. Direct appropriations should be substituted for these special pipelines to the Treasury.

8. *Use a "budget scorecard."* Until it adopts more fundamental reforms (such as those suggested above), the Congress should use a "budget scorecard" to show the cumulative effects of individual budget decisions on the overall budget aggregates. This mechanism would enable each congressional committee that is reviewing a given item to treat it as the marginal case. At the least, the scorecard would provide an up-to-date recording of the impact of congressional action on the overall fiscal picture.

9. *Improve program analysis and evaluation.* The essential ingredient in any proposal for controlling expenditures is critical evaluation of federal programs and agency expenditure requests. Evaluative research is now a virtual monopoly of the executive branch, to the extent that it is used at all. If Congress is ever to oversee executive administration effectively, then it needs professional assistance beyond that provided by existing committee staffs. As imperfect as evaluation techniques are, at the least they would be a useful supplement to existing rules-of-thumb and other subjective approaches. In addition, critical analyses of agency budget justifications by the GAO should be made available for oversight and appropriations hearings.

An Office of Program Analysis and Evaluation, established in the General Accounting Office with a nonpartisan staff, could provide objective analytical studies of program costs, benefits, and alternatives, both for existing and proposed undertakings.

The Outlook

At the present time in the United States, there appears to be a log jam in the process of policy formulation. On budget and many other domestic policies, the President and the Congress are close to an impasse. On tax reform, a stalemate seems to be developing between the advocates of change designed to eliminate alleged inequities and the defenders of provisions that many consider necessary incentives to private endeavors.

The outlook is for a period of strained relations between the Congress and the executive branch. This is a situation which makes ambitious new spending or sweeping tax reforms unlikely. In fact, cutbacks in government programs—or to put it more precisely, slow-downs in their growth rates—could be the order of the day. Given rapid economic expansion and continued inflationary pressures, these budget results appear to be consistent with the needs of economic policy.

This report suggests relatively modest but forward looking changes that perhaps will redirect the public and governmental debate along more practical lines. Looking beyond the immediate scene, we can envision a time when—as a result of the success of the current economy efforts in reducing the base of the budget—new expenditure initiatives, albeit of modest proportions, may become feasible within the confines of the revenue growth from existing taxes. New interest in evaluating existing public undertakings may identify more effective approaches for dealing with the difficult social, economic, and ecological problems that we have today.

Part One:
Economic Analyses

2
THE BUDGET FOR FISCAL 1974

If government spending can be held in check, the federal government can operate a responsible fiscal policy in fiscal year 1974 without an increase in taxes. This is the dominant theme in President Nixon's new budget.

As in the last several years, the budget defines a responsible fiscal policy as a balance in the so-called full-employment budget. Thus, if unemployment were to average 4 percent of the labor force in fiscal 1974—which is not the same as forecasting that unemployment actually will average 4 percent—it is estimated that federal revenues would be $300 million higher than federal outlays.

It is interesting to note that the 4 percent figure is still used as the definition of "full" employment in these calculations, even though the likelihood of reaching that level has become quite remote, at least in the absence of expanded manpower and other labor market programs. Clearly, if full employment were redefined as, say 4½ percent unemployment, as some have suggested, then the degree of fiscal restraint required to ensure that the economy does not become overheated would be greater than the restraint proposed in the new budget.

In any event, examination of the budgetary details will show how difficult even the current objective will be to achieve. Table 1 indicates how readily that slim full-employment surplus of $300 million could be converted to a full-employment deficit. Merely the addition of the widely discussed reconstruction program for Vietnam—or, alternatively, national health insurance or any other substantial program—could prevent attainment of the full-employment balance. And in the current environment of legislative-executive tension, it is not likely that the Congress will grant all of the President's requests for special legislation enabling him to reduce the programs of the Department of

Health, Education and Welfare (HEW) and Veterans Administration by over $1.4 billion in fiscal 1974. (Reports that the administration is reconsidering the proposed cuts in veterans pensions suggest another way the surplus could slip away.)

Table 1
POSSIBLE "OVERRUNS" IN THE FULL-EMPLOYMENT BUDGET
(fiscal year 1974, $ in millions)

Estimated full-employment surplus	300
Deduct: outlay savings requiring congressional action	1,436
Resultant full-employment deficit	− 1,136
Deduct: Southeast Asia reconstruction	1,000
Resultant full-employment deficit	− 2,136
Deduct: federal share of new health insurance program	500
Resultant full-employment deficit	− 2,636

Alternatives to above possibilities: Property tax relief for the elderly; Equalizing public school financing; Welfare reform; Other congressional initiatives.

Indeed, there are many other uncertainties that must work out correctly if the full-employment budget balance is to be achieved: not only must both the President and the Congress refrain from major new spending initiatives, but the departments and agencies must also achieve the numerous program economies and efficiencies promised in the new budget, both those requiring direct congressional approval and those entirely within the discretion of the executive branch. Judging from the experience of the last several years, it is far easier to project a full-employment balance in the federal budget, than to actually attain it. Similar projections of a slim surplus in the full-employment budget were presented in the two previous budgets, and events converted the estimated surpluses to deficits. On a full-employment basis, the budget showed a $3.9 billion deficit in the fiscal year 1972, and a $2.3 billion deficit is now estimated for fiscal 1973.

Nevertheless, it does seem clear that the efforts by the Nixon administration are likely to result in a lower level of federal spending than would otherwise be the case. Given the rapid growth in economic activity that is now taking place and the concern over a rebirth of inflationary pressures, such an outcome would certainly be consistent with the needs of economic policy.

The Economic Rationale

The key basis on which the Nixon administration can predict a major reduction in the federal deficit from fiscal 1973 to fiscal 1974 is the strong economic expansion that is expected to continue at least through the calendar year 1973 (see Table 2). The administration's

Table 2
ECONOMIC ASSUMPTIONS UNDERLYING THE BUDGET FOR FISCAL 1974
($ in billions)

	Calendar Years			Percent Increase 1972-73
	1971 Actual	1972 Preliminary	1973 Estimate	
Gross national product	1,050	1,152	1,267	10.0%
Personal income	861	936	1,018	8.8
Corporate profits before tax	83	94	108	14.9

projection of a $1,267 billion gross national product for 1973 is well within the range of projections made by experienced private forecasters, although at the higher end of the range. In fact, the "standard" forecast for the year's GNP has been raised from $1,260 billion—which was the prevailing view last fall—to at least $1,265 billion. The economic boom clearly is continuing to pick up steam. Last year's projection of GNP—$1,145 billion for calendar year 1972—was also considered to be optimistic at the time it was presented, but it turned out to be $7 billion below the (preliminary) actual figure for the year.

For policy purposes, the administration has adopted a target of 3 percent inflation in terms of the GNP deflator for calendar year 1973. (This would translate into a 2½ percent increase in the consumer price index.) In contrast, most private forecasts are higher, in the vicinity of 3½ percent. Since the announcement of Phase III, a number of private forecasters have raised their inflation forecasts from somewhat below 3½ percent to a bit above that figure. The administration is aware of this. It frankly admits in the January 1973 *Report of the Council of Economic Advisers* that the attainment of its inflation objective will require a high degree of compliance with Phase III, as well as success in keeping food prices down. The slim prospect of keeping inflation down to the 3 percent rate reinforces the case for greater fiscal restraint.

The Budget Totals

The unified budget projects receipts of $256.0 billion and outlays of $268.7 billion in fiscal 1974. The estimated deficit for the next fiscal year is thus $12.7 billion, about half of the 1973 deficit. This substantial reduction in the deficit is the result of strong growth in revenues (which is implied by the economic assumptions discussed above) and the continuation of expenditure restraint begun in the fiscal year 1973 (see Table 3). Continued expenditure restraint will

Table 3
RECEIPTS AND OUTLAYS UNDER THREE BUDGET MEASUREMENTS
(fiscal years 1972-74, $ in millions)

	1972 Actual	1973 Estimate	1974 Estimate
Unified budget			
Receipts	208.6	225.0	256.0
Outlays	231.9	249.8	268.7
Deficit (−)	− 23.2	− 24.8	− 12.7
Federal transactions in the national accounts			
Receipts	211.9	233.3	263.0
Expenditures	233.1	259.9	275.5
Excess of expenditures (−)	− 21.1	− 26.6	− 12.5
Full employment budget			
Receipts	225.0	245.0	268.0
Outlays	228.9	247.3	267.7
Surplus (+) or deficit (−)	− 3.9	− 2.3	+ 0.3

be influenced, of course, by the outcome of the struggle for dominance—which is now beginning to heat up—between the White House and the Congress.

Outlays for fiscal 1974 are projected to rise by $19 billion or 7.5 percent above this year's level—which, in turn, was $18 billion or 7.7 percent above the fiscal 1972 figure. There has been much rhetoric about "slashes" and cutbacks in federal outlays. While there have been cutbacks in some federal programs, in general the reality is more in the way of a modest slowdown in the rate of growth of government spending. Moreover, the expenditure figures for both fiscal 1973 and fiscal 1974 contain a good deal of optimism concerning the administration's ability to effectuate quick and substantial improvements in the efficiency of government operations. The budget contains numerous vague references to efforts to "Tighten operations of revolving and management funds" (thereby saving $200 million in the Department of Defense), "Strengthen Medicaid management" (for a $175 million saving), "Increase efficiencies of Coast Guard operations" (reducing spending by $10 million), and so on. No information is provided as to how these improvements will be made. Moreover, 1974 outlays will be $1.4 billion higher than shown in Table 3 unless the Congress passes legislation reducing Medicare, social security, and other specific welfare benefits. The likelihood of congressional cooperation on these matters is not great.

One shortcoming of the new budget concerns programs not included in that document. There is no allowance for, nor any mention of, the reconstruction program for Southeast Asia that has figured so prominently in the cease-fire discussions. Earlier estimates of the cost of such a program were in the neighborhood of $7 billion over a five-year period. Although the cost will probably be shared by other countries, the resultant burden on the U.S. Treasury is expected to be large. In contrast to the "peace dividend" that the public has anticipated from the end of the Vietnam War, a large liability is now more likely.

Also absent from the budget are the major domestic initiatives which last year's presidential messages indicated were being developed for "relieving the burden of property taxes and providing fair and adequate financing for our children's education." The most modest of the proposals for property tax relief or for equalizing the financing of public schools would require federal outlays on the order of a billion dollars or more a year.

For example, it has been suggested that, with an annual outlay of about $1.25 billion, the federal government can "hurry history along" by encouraging the states to establish broad-gauged "circuit-breaker" systems on their property taxes. Under such an arrangement, a reduction or refund on the state income tax would be provided to all low-income homeowners and renters to help offset the burden of property taxes. Some have also urged a limited and temporary federal assistance program designed to encourage the states to move more rapidly toward the objective of placing their local school districts on a more equal fiscal footing. A new federal program providing $20-$40 per school-age child could involve an additional cost to the U.S. Treasury of $1-$2 billion a year.

Clearly, for the time being, the administration has concluded that the alternative of avoiding a federal tax increase is more consistent with the desires of the public. To the extent that the current economy efforts are successful in reducing the base of the budget, some new expenditure initiatives of modest proportions, within the confines of the revenue growth from existing taxes, may become feasible in subsequent years.

The Changing Composition of Spending

Compared to the last few years, the 1974 budget shows a relative stability in the shares of the budget devoted to the major functional areas. The portion of the budget devoted to national defense, after declining from 41 percent in 1970, is stabilizing at about 30 percent. Similarly, human resource programs (such as education, health, and income security), after a rapid rise from 37 percent in 1970, are leveling off at 47 percent of total federal spending. Apparently the shift in priorities from "warfare" to "welfare" in government outlays has been virtually completed. Most other changes are of a much smaller magnitude. The most significant has been the new general revenue sharing program, which now accounts for 2 percent of total budget expenditures. Federal outlays by function are shown in Table 4 and are discussed below.

National defense. Total outlays for Department of Defense and related activities in the national defense category are budgeted for an increase of $4.7 billion for fiscal 1974 over 1973. This represents a reversal from the pattern of the last several years; national defense spending declined almost $5 billion from $81.2 billion in fiscal 1969— the Vietnam peak—to $76.4 billion estimated for fiscal 1973.

The bulk of the budgeted increase, $4.1 billion, is allocated for the following uses: to maintain military and civilian pay levels comparable to those in the private sector, to raise pay and benefit levels sufficient to achieve an all-volunteer armed force, to meet price increases in military purchases, and to pay for higher military retirement annuities. Moreover, if Congress follows the same procedure with the 1974 budget that it did with the 1973 budget, a cut in the defense budget in the neighborhood of $3 billion may be expected. Thus, there is little likelihood of increased defense spending in real terms.

In an attempt to check the past trend of rising manpower costs, the new budget devotes major emphasis to equipment modernization and R&D. The proportion of the defense budget devoted to manpower costs is estimated to stay at the 1973 level, about 56 percent,

Table 4

SUMMARY OF BUDGET OUTLAYS BY FUNCTION, FISCAL YEARS 1972-74

($ in millions)

Function	1972 Actual	1973 Estimate	1974 Estimate
National defense [a]	78,336	76,435	81,074
International affairs and finance	3,726	3,341	3,811
Space research and technology	3,422	3,061	3,135
Agricultural and rural development	7,063	6,064	5,572
Natural resources and environment	3,761	876	3,663
Commerce and transportation	11,201	12,543	11,580
Community development and housing	4,282	3,957	4,931
Education and manpower	9,751	10,500	10,110
Health	17,112	17,991	21,730
Income security	64,876	75,889	81,976
Veterans benefits and services	10,731	11,795	11,732
Interest	20,582	22,808	24,672
General government	4,891	5,631	6,025
General revenue sharing	—	6,786	6,035
Allowances for contingencies and civilian agency pay raises	—	500	1,750
Undistributed intragovernmental transactions:			
Employer share, employee retirement	− 2,768	− 2,980	− 3,157
Interest received by trust funds	− 5,089	− 5,401	− 5,974
Total budget outlays	231,876	249,796	268,665

[a] Includes allowances for all-volunteer force, retirement systems reform, and civilian and military pay raises for Department of Defense.

after a sharp rise from 42 percent in 1968. Apparently, the large increases in military pay needed to attract sufficient volunteers already have occurred; the recent announcement of the cessation of draft calls would appear to confirm that.

Three strategic weapons programs figure prominently in the new budget: (1) continued development of the Trident sea-based ballistic missile system (intended to replace the Polaris), (2) further development of the B-1 advanced long-range bomber (replacing the B-52), and (3) additional conversions of existing Minuteman and Polaris forces to MIRV configurations (multiple independently targeted warheads). The so-called blue water strategy is also evident in the general purpose forces. Fiscal 1974 money is provided for five nuclear-powered submarines, a nuclear-powered aircraft carrier, and the modernization of three guided-missile frigates. Pursuant to the Strategic Arms Limitation Treaty (SALT), work has stopped on the second ABM site in Malmstrom, Montana. No funds are included for deployment of an ABM defense of Washington, D. C., which is permitted under SALT-1.

As shown in Table 5, projected outlay savings of approximately $2.7 billion are anticipated in the national defense category in the fiscal year 1974. These will come from a variety of program reductions in

Table 5
PROJECTED OUTLAY SAVINGS IN NATIONAL DEFENSE
(fiscal year 1974, $ in millions)

Agency and Program	Estimated Savings
Department of Defense–military:	
Reduce personnel and other operating costs	1,200
Reduce procurement of Safeguard, aircraft, missiles, and ships	650
Limit growth in research, development, test, and evaluation programs	200
Reduce construction for Safeguard and housing	50
Limit new spending for All-Volunteer Force and other legislation	400
Tighten operations of revolving and management funds	200
Total, Department of Defense-military	2,700
Atomic Energy Commission:	
Reduce Plowshare program to permit further study	3
Reduce space electric power and propulsion program	12
Defer projects in nuclear materials, civilian reactor and research program	21
Reduce inventory and working capital requirements [a]	−35
Total, Atomic Energy Commission	1
Total, national defense	2,701

[a] Offsetting savings of $56 million are anticipated in fiscal year 1973.

the Department of Defense and the Atomic Energy Commission. However, from the limited detail presented in the budget, it is difficult to determine what specific actions will be required to achieve many of these savings or what the implications of such actions will be. In the case of the Safeguard, presumably the reductions result from SALT which requires the United States to stop work on the ABM site in Montana.

One indication of the buildup of future pressures on the level of military outlays is the extent to which new budget authority is in excess of the current flow of expenditures. In the fiscal year 1973, it is expected that the fiscal "pipeline" of the Pentagon will be enhanced by an excess of $3.6 billion of new authority over current outlays; in 1974 this increment is estimated at $5.2 billion.

International affairs and finance. This category, which finances foreign economic aid and State Department functions, shows a rise of $470 million from 1973 to 1974. The bulk of the increase results from an accounting reason—a reduction of $361 million in proprietary receipts from the public. Smaller rises are projected for defense related economic aid ($145 million) and multilateral development assistance ($115 million). The estimated 1974 outlays of $3,811 million for international affairs and finance assume that a saving of $62 million will be achieved by reducing programs (not designated) of the Agency for International Development below levels previously budgeted.

Any Vietnam reconstruction program would be funded in this program category. The official explanation usually given is that the new program will be financed by further reductions in other programs. Expenditure estimates of existing foreign aid programs are usually inflated to allow for the possibility of cuts by the Congress. Should those cuts be made, equivalent spending on the Vietnam program could be funded within the existing budget total.

Space research and technology. After an almost steady decline from a peak of approximately $6 billion in fiscal 1966, outlays for civilian space programs are leveling off at an annual level of about $3 billion. The major new initiative, the manned reusable space shuttle, is now to be carried forward at a more leisurely pace than envisioned earlier. In calendar 1973, Skylab, a three-man experimental space station, will test man's ability to live and work in space for up to 56 days.

As shown in Table 6, a reduction of $251 million in outlays for space programs is estimated to result from a number of specific and general cutbacks. The largest, $68 million, is deferring the high-energy astronomy observatory in order to provide the National Aeronautics and Space Administration with an opportunity to see if the same objectives could be achieved at lower cost. But, presumably, NASA was supposed to have considered such alternatives prior to going ahead with the observatory in the first place.

Agriculture and rural development. The combination of a lessened need for farm price supports and cutbacks in several specific programs, partially offset by some increases, is expected to reduce total outlays for agriculture and rural development from $6.1 billion this

Table 6

PROJECTED OUTLAY SAVINGS IN SPACE RESEARCH
AND TECHNOLOGY

(fiscal year 1974, $ in millions)

Agency and Program	Estimated Savings
National Aeronautics and Space Administration:	
Delay space shuttle	45
Reduce other manned space flight	47
Defer high-energy astronomy observatory	68
Cancel application technology satellite-G	17
Reduce nuclear power and propulsion research	16
Cancel experimental STOL aircraft	34
Reduce NASA personnel and administrative expenses	24
Total, NASA and space research and technology	251

year to $5.6 billion in fiscal 1974. A total of 20 million acres, a third of the land idle in 1972, is scheduled to be returned to production in 1973; it is anticipated that this action will yield sufficient private farm income to reduce the need for subsidies. The demand for farm products is bright; agricultural exports are projected at $10 billion in 1973, almost $2 billion above the all-time high reached last year.

A temporary halt has been declared on accepting new loan and grant applications under subsidized housing programs of the Department of Agriculture. The budget proposes that loans for electric and telephone service in rural areas be shifted from a direct to an insured basis beginning in 1973. Thus, the trend toward financing more activities outside of the budget proper is continuing.

Table 7 lists the $1.9 billion savings anticipated from cutting back some farm programs. The bulk of the reduction in outlays results from the reduced need for farm price supports due to rapidly rising domestic and foreign demand for food, rather than from any deliberate or discretionary cutback in federal farm programs. Smaller but more discretionary savings result from long-overdue terminations of subsidies going back to the New Deal days, such as eliminating federal payments to private individuals for improving the soil and water management practices which benefit their own lands. Similarly, the 5 percent interest to be charged on the new insured loans by the rural development insurance fund of the Farmers Home Administration is far more realistic than the 2 percent rate—well below what the Treasury itself must pay to borrow money—that applied to direct loans by the Rural Electrification Administration (REA).

Table 7

PROJECTED OUTLAY SAVINGS IN AGRICULTURE
AND RURAL DEVELOPMENT
(fiscal year 1974, $ in millions)

Agency and Program	Estimated Savings
Department of Agriculture:	
Reduce cost of farm price supports	1,219
Shift rural electrification from direct to insured loans	373
Eliminate cost-sharing for soil and water management practices on private lands	258
Curtail anticipated growth in agriculture extension programs and reduce support for agricultural research	34
Total, Department of Agriculture	1,884

Natural resources and environment. The fundamental shift underway in the composition of this budget category is currently obscured by sharp fluctuations in the rents and royalties being obtained from the outer continental shelf lands (these program receipts are treated as negative expenditures). The revenues from the off-shore leases are expected to decline from a peak of $4.2 billion in 1973 to $2.1 billion in 1974. Much of this reflects a one-time payment out of escrow funds, as a result of a recent court order.

In terms of substantive programs, the most rapid rise occurs in estimated outlays for pollution control and abatement, which almost treble from $762 million in 1972 to $2.1 billion in 1974. Expenditures for the more conventional Corps of Engineers and Bureau of Reclamation water resources and power projects are estimated to decline from $3.1 billion in 1973 to $2.8 billion in 1974.

Table 8 shows the many cutbacks scheduled by the administration in the natural resources and environment area. If these actions are not taken, the expansion in this total category would proceed at a far more rapid rate than is now estimated in the budget. The list of cutbacks seems somewhat overblown. About $1 billion of the $2.4 billion of what the budget labels "program reductions and terminations" results from the happy, if not fortuitous, situation that sales of leases on the outer continental shelf seem to be proceeding at a more rapid rate than was envisioned earlier. The second largest saving ($950 million) results from the President's determination not to spend all of the pollution control funds made available by the Congress. The administration argues that capacity is not available to build sewage treatment plants at the rate envisioned by the Congress and that, therefore,

Table 8

PROJECTED OUTLAY SAVINGS IN NATURAL RESOURCES
AND ENVIRONMENT

(fiscal year 1974, $ in millions)

Agency and Program	Estimated Savings
Department of Agriculture:	
Terminate rural water systems and waste disposal grants which are replaced by loans	100
Achieve economies in the Forest Service through tightened management, reduced state forestry support, and shifting construction of forest roads to timber purchasers	94
Total, Department of Agriculture	194
Department of Defense–civil:	
Slow scheduling of navigation and flood control projects	471
Department of the Interior:	
Reduce construction activity in national parks, public lands, and Indian areas to less than anticipated rates	10
Schedule some Bureau of Reclamation projects at less than anticipated rates	123
Deemphasize construction of large-scale saline water test plants of known technology	14
Constrain land purchases for recreation and wildlife areas below anticipated levels	61
Increase rate of lease sales on Outer Continental Shelf	1,010
Reduce other costs	2
Total, Department of the Interior	1,220
Environmental Protection Agency:	
Actions related to Federal Water Pollution Control Act Amendments of 1972	950
Tennessee Valley Authority:	
Slow construction activity	30
Total, natural resources and environment	2,865

spending at that rate would only serve to increase the prices that the government will be paying.

The cutbacks in the projects of the Corps of Engineers and Bureau of Reclamation is likely to be welcomed by economists and ecologists who have maintained for years that many of these projects do not make a positive contribution to the nation's economic growth or welfare. Indeed when proper allowance is made for the cost of capital and the adverse environmental effects, many of these undertakings cost the nation far more than any benefits that they may yield.

Commerce and transportation. Total outlays for commerce and transportation are projected to decline from $12.5 billion in 1973 to $11.6 billion in 1974. Although the Budget Message does not so state, it appears that virtually the entire reduction results from the very reasonable assumption that a disaster of the magnitude of tropical storm Agnes will not recur in 1974 (the one-shot disbursements for disaster relief for the victims of that storm came to about $1 billion). An estimated decline of $337 million in federal subsidies to the Postal Service offsets smaller increases in various transportation programs. In addition, a large number of individually small program reductions are anticipated with cumulative savings of $417 million in fiscal 1974 (see Table 9).

Table 9
PROJECTED OUTLAY SAVINGS IN COMMERCE AND TRANSPORTATION
(fiscal year 1974, $ in millions)

Agency and Program	Estimated Savings
Department of Commerce:	
Phase out Economic Development Administration programs	35
Redirect or defer R&D programs of National Oceanic and Atmospheric Administration	41
Limit planned expansion of National Bureau of Standards science and technology programs	10
Eliminate federal participation in regional commissions	27
Total, Department of Commerce	113
Department of Transportation:	
States are deferring highway projects	83
Defer some Coast Guard construction and research	14
Reschedule FAA equipment purchase and long-range research	35
Defer high-speed rail R&D	41
Reduce operating subsidies for Amtrak	27
Hold up hardware contracts for Urban Mass Transit for additional study	26
Reduce R&D projects on intermodal transport	7
Increase efficiency of Coast Guard operations	10
Increase efficiency of FAA operations	20
Total, Department of Transportation	263
Small Business Administration:	
Shift some direct loans to guarantees of private lending	41
Total, commerce and transportation	417

Community development and housing. Despite the recently announced freeze on many new federal housing programs, total outlays for community development and housing are projected to rise from $4.0 billion in 1973 to $4.9 billion in 1974. This continued increase results from the commitments already in the pipeline for low-rent public housing, rent supplements, home ownership assistance, and rental housing assistance. Savings of $312 million are anticipated in 1974, mainly from temporarily suspending new commitments under housing subsidy programs and discontinuing federal funding of community action organizations (see Table 10). In contrast, new budget authority for this entire category is estimated to decline from $5.9 billion in 1973 to $3.9 billion in 1974. The bulk of federal assistance to housing and home owners will continue to be in the form of credit aids, such as mortgage guarantees, which are not included in the budget.

Table 10
PROJECTED OUTLAY SAVINGS IN COMMUNITY DEVELOPMENT AND HOUSING
(fiscal year 1974, $ in millions)

Agency and Program	Estimated Savings
Office of Economic Opportunity:	
Reassign OEO activities and discontinue federal funding of community action organizations	328
Department of Housing and Urban Development:	
Suspend new commitments under housing subsidy programs	305
Terminate categorical community development programs in favor of urban special revenue sharing	7
Total, Department of HUD	312
Total, community development and housing	640

Education and manpower. For the first time in at least a decade, the rapid rise in federal spending for education and manpower appears to halt in 1974, when outlays decline slightly from the 1973 level of $10.5 billion to a projected $10.1 billion. However, if the data are disaggregated, no overall cutbacks are visible in either education or manpower training. The reduction in the total category is more than accounted for by the phasing out of the emergency employment assistance program begun in 1972.

Expenditure savings of $264 million are anticipated in fiscal year 1974 from substituting governmental guarantees of student loans for the existing program of direct federal loans. This is another move toward "debudgeting" federal credit programs. Total savings for the year in education and manpower are projected at $1.7 billion (see Table 11), mostly from cutting back the emergency state and local employment program. The improvements in the national job situation and in state-local finances would seem to make this move feasible.

Table 11
PROJECTED OUTLAY SAVINGS IN EDUCATION AND MANPOWER
(fiscal year 1974, $ in millions)

Agency and Program	Estimated Savings
Department of Health, Education, and Welfare:	
Substitute education revenue sharing for—	
Foreign language and area training	13
Land grant college support	10
University community services	15
State departments of education	36
Payments to local school systems in "impacted" areas	119
Public school libraries	49
Certain "narrowly focused" categorical programs	53
Substitute private market for federal capitalization of direct student loans	264
Total, Department of HEW	559
Department of Labor:	
Reform manpower training programs	354
Phase down Emergency Employment Assistance program	670
Increase efficiency of employment and unemployment insurance services	35
Tighten operations and management	10
Total, Department of Labor	1,069
National Science Foundation:	
Curtail some institutional and educational programs and other reductions	32
Total, education and manpower	1,660

Health. Continued growth in the cost of Medicare and Medicaid accounts for almost all of the projected $3.7 billion rise in federal outlays for health from fiscal year 1973 to 1974. The Nixon administration repeats its earlier recommendation for a national health insurance program, although no funds for the purpose are visible in the budget. Presumably, the bulk of the cost would be borne by employers and employees in the form of premium payments to private insurance carriers. Nevertheless, most proposals for national health insurance (such as the one made by the administration last year) include some allowance for direct federal payments in the case of low-income wage earners and employees of very small businesses.

Were it not for the various economies anticipated in the budget (see Table 12), the projected increase in federal health spending in

Table 12
PROJECTED OUTLAY SAVINGS IN HEALTH
(fiscal year 1974, $ in millions)

Agency and Program	Estimated Savings
Proposed actions not requiring substantive legislation	
Department of Health, Education, and Welfare:	
Strengthen Medicare cost controls and eliminate unnecessary advance payments for hospitals	277
Strengthen Medicaid management	175
Eliminate medical facilities grants and regional medical program	189
Phase out federal financing for local mental health programs	63
Eliminate duplicative health program grants	53
Phase out training grants and control level of non-priority research grants	57
Focus health manpower training support on areas of special need	49
Subtotal	863
Proposed actions requiring substantive legislation	
Eliminate federal financing for low-priority Medicaid services to adults	75
Reform Medicare cost-sharing and implement effective utilization review	616
Subtotal	691
Total, health	1,554

fiscal 1974 would be $5.2 billion instead of $3.7 billion. Of the $1,554 million anticipated economies, $691 million require the passage of substantive legislation by the Congress. The balance, $863 million in administrative savings, stands a better chance of being achieved, provided these savings are not offset by the overruns in Medicare and Medicaid benefits that have been so characteristic in recent years.

Income security. Primarily as a result of the generous 20 percent increase in social security benefits enacted by the 92nd Congress, outlays for income security programs are anticipated to rise from $75.9 billion this year to $82.0 billion in 1974. The effort to reform the welfare programs—which has repeatedly been rejected by the Congress—is being abandoned by the administration, at least for the time being. Nevertheless, federal public assistance expenditures rise substantially because, effective January 1, 1974, the federal government will assume full responsibility for providing basic assistance for the "adult" categories—the aged, blind, and disabled.

Table 13 sets forth the administration's claimed savings in the income security category in fiscal 1974. The largest item, however—$2.7 billion in reduced outlays for social services grants—is not something the executive branch can claim sole credit for: the reductions

Table 13
PROJECTED OUTLAY SAVINGS IN INCOME SECURITY
(fiscal year 1974, $ in millions)

Agency and Program	Estimated Savings
Proposed actions not requiring substantive legislation	
Department of Agriculture:	
Limit special milk subsidy to institutions not otherwise receiving subsidized milk	59
Department of Health, Education, and Welfare:	
Limit outlays on social services grants	2,700
Adjust growth rate for vocational rehabilitation	31
Limit to 5 years federal funding for Cuban refugees	58
Institute quality control for social services, research, and training	31
Eliminate overpayments and payments to ineligible recipients of public assistance and introduce management improvements	592
Subtotal, Department of HEW	3,412
Department of Labor:	
Allocate proper unemployment benefit costs to Postal Service	26
Civil Service Commission:	
Allocate proper retirement costs to Postal Service	285
Proposed actions requiring substantive legislation	
Eliminate certain optional payment procedures under OASDI	310
Improve structure of public assistance programs	158
Subtotal	468
Total, income security	4,250

were mandated by the Congress, an action which the administration supported. The $311 million of costs to be allocated to the Postal Service will presumably require an increase in postal rates or some offsetting economy; however, those transactions would not show up in the budget. Of the $4,250 million of projected economies in income security, $468 million require passage of special legislation by the Congress before they become effective.

Veterans benefits and services. As a result of several administrative reforms and proposed legislation, total outlays for veterans programs are projected to decline slightly from $11.8 billion in 1973 to $11.7 billion in 1974. If Congress does not go along with the President's plans to eliminate duplicate burial payments and reduce certain pension payments, outlays in 1974 may be $277 million higher than shown in the budget (see Table 14). As pointed out earlier, the administration is reconsidering some of these proposed cuts.

Table 14
PROJECTED OUTLAY SAVINGS IN VETERANS BENEFITS AND SERVICES
(fiscal year 1974, $ in millions)

Agency and Program	Estimated Savings
Proposed actions not requiring substantive legislation	
Veterans Administration:	
Reform veterans benefits to align benefits and need	160
Reschedule construction activities	55
Restructure research in line with current needs	13
Subtotal	228
Proposed actions requiring substantive legislation	
Eliminate duplicate burial benefits	54
Bring pensions into closer alignment with need	223
Subtotal	277
Total, Veterans Administration	505

Interest. Consistent with yet another rise in the federal debt, interest payments are projected to increase from $22.8 billion in 1973 to $24.7 billion in 1974. Of the $24.7 billion in interest payments, $6.0 billion will be paid to trust funds and other government investment accounts. Hence, the net outlays for interest to the public will be $18.7 billion in 1974, approximately $1.3 billion higher than in the current year.

General government. Overhead and multi-functional programs, budgeted under the category general government, are estimated at $6.0 billion in 1974 compared to $5.6 billion in 1973. The largest increase—$247 million—occurs in the law enforcement area. As the President indicated, the size of the executive office is being reduced by more than 50 percent. The decline in personnel is being achieved by eliminating agencies such as the Office of Economic Opportunity and the Office of Emergency Preparedness, as well as by cutting personnel in some of the remaining units. The Council of Economic Advisers is scheduled for a 20 percent reduction in staff size. Other economies are shown in Table 15.

Table 15
PROJECTED OUTLAY SAVINGS IN GENERAL GOVERNMENT
(fiscal year 1974, $ in millions)

Agency and Program	Estimated Savings
Department of Justice:	
Review prison construction program	28
Return responsibility to agencies for Community Relations Service technical assistance program	4
Total, Department of Justice	32
Department of the Treasury:	
Delay construction of Federal Law Enforcement Training Center	12
Reduce personnel, travel, and related costs	9
Total, Department of the Treasury	21
General Services Administration:	
Provide more efficient guard service in public buildings	3
Require more effective supply practices	25
Reduce new computer procurement	9
Total, General Services Administration	37
Civil Service Commission:	
Limit intergovernmental personnel assistance grants	1
Washington Metropolitan Area Transit Authority:	
Use bond proceeds to even out federal contribution	13
Total, general government	104

General revenue sharing. Because the revenue sharing disbursements to state and local governments in the fiscal year 1973 contained a large retroactive payment, total outlays in the program are estimated to decline by $800 million in 1974 to a total of $6.0 billion. In four of the functional areas discussed earlier, the Nixon administration has developed plans for consolidating some of the wide variety of categorical grants-in-aid into "special revenue sharing" programs. When fully effective, about $6.9 billion is expected to be disbursed to state and local governments in this fashion for urban community development, education, manpower training, and law enforcement.

With all the talk of cutbacks in categorical aid, it is easy to lose sight of the facts that the great bulk of federal aid to state and local governments will continue to be made in the form of categorical grants and that this form of aid continues to rise. Thus, total federal outlays for grants-in-aid are projected to rise from $38.2 billion in fiscal year 1973 to $38.8 billion in 1974. The reality in this area appears to be more in the nature of a slowdown in what has been a most rapid rate of growth in the last few years.

Federal Credit Programs. It is estimated that $26.9 billion of credit will be advanced to the public under federal auspices in 1974 (see Table 16). This amount exceeds the total outlays budgeted for the legislative and judicial branches, the Executive Office of the President, and the Departments of Agriculture, Commerce, Housing and Urban Development, Interior, Justice, Labor and State. Yet, of this $26.9 billion of credit activity, only the $0.9 billion of direct federal loans is included in the unified budget totals.

The practice of excluding loan insurance and sponsored agency loan programs from the budget provides an incentive to shift from direct outlays to these programs in order to reduce the budget deficit. Table 17 details the proposed shifts out of the budget of four programs and the effects of these shifts on the fiscal 1974 budget totals.

Table 16
NET CREDIT ADVANCED TO THE PUBLIC
UNDER FEDERAL AUSPICES
(fiscal years, $ in billions)

Type of Credit Assistance	1972 Actual	1973 Estimate	1974 Estimate
Direct federal loans	2.7	−0.1	0.9
Guaranteed loans	14.9	17.2	13.8
Loans of federally sponsored agencies	4.4	10.7	12.2
Total	22.0	27.8	26.9

Table 17
SHIFTING DIRECT EXPENDITURES TO NON-BUDGET CREDIT PROGRAMS
($ in millions)

Agency and Program	Savings in Fiscal 1974 Outlays
Department of Agriculture:	
Shift Rural Electrification from direct to insured loans	258
Department of Health, Education, and Welfare:	
Substitute private for federal capital for student loans	264
Small Business Administration:	
Shift from direct to guaranteed private loans	41
Washington Metropolitan Area Transit Authority:	
Use bond proceeds to reduce federal contribution	13
Total	576

Long-term direct loans of the Rural Electrification Administration at 2 percent interest are to be terminated, effective January 1, 1973. In their place, the Farmers Home Administration is to provide insurance for private loans (at 5 percent interest) under the rural development insurance fund. Total program increases of $200 million are projected for both 1973 and 1974.

No new funds are contained in the budget for federal capital contributions to the national direct student loan program. Instead, the need is expected to be filled by increases in federally insured loans, expanded work-study programs, and the proposed "basic opportunity grant" (which would make any student eligible for a grant of up to $1,400 or one-half of the cost of his education). Extra-budgetary student aid is also to be supplied by the new Student Loan Marketing Association, Sally Mae, which is scheduled to begin operations in 1974 as a federally sponsored agency providing a secondary market for insured student loans.

Shifting expenditures out of the budget, of course, removes these programs from budgetary discipline; as a result, extra-budgetary credit programs tend to grow at a much faster rate than budgeted items. The Export-Import Bank, for example, was removed from the budget in fiscal 1972; in that year its net lending was only $0.3 billion. In 1973, Eximbank's net lending jumped almost 500 percent to $1.7 billion, and approximately this level of activity is projected for 1974.

Most major credit programs contain some element of subsidy. This subsidy arises from the fact that loans are made at rates below those that the Treasury itself must pay to borrow money. The present value of the subsidies in direct and guaranteed loans in fiscal 1974 is estimated to be $2.5 billion, down from $7.0 billion in FY 1972 and $4.8 billion in the current year. Almost all of this decrease can be traced to the reduction or elimination of guaranteed loans by the Department of Housing and Urban Development, especially subsidized mortgage insurance and guarantees for low-rent public housing, and to the phasing out of REA 2 percent loans and the sharp cutback in the student loan program.

Financing Expenditures

Budget receipts. The budget for fiscal 1974 estimates receipts of $256.0 billion, an increase of $31 billion or 14 percent from this fiscal year (see Table 18). This expected rise in revenue reflects mainly the expected improvement in the economic situation and the resulting expansion of the tax base. Legislative changes affecting receipts are minor and virtually offsetting. In the current fiscal year, in contrast, the growth in receipts is being held down by the legislative changes contained in the Revenue Act of 1971.

Individual income taxes are estimated at $111.6 billion in 1974, an increase of $12.2 billion over 1973. This growth is largely due to

Table 18
BUDGET RECEIPTS BY SOURCE
(fiscal years, $ in millions)

Category of Receipts	1972 Actual	1973 Estimate	1974 Estimate
Individual income taxes	94,737	99,400	111,600
Corporation income taxes	32,166	33,500	37,000
Social insurance taxes and contributions	53,914	64,540	78,162
Excise taxes	15,477	15,970	16,798
Estate and gift taxes	5,436	4,600	5,000
Customs duties	3,287	3,000	3,300
Miscellaneous receipts	3,633	3,975	4,122
Total	208,649	224,984	255,982

the anticipated rise in taxable personal income. Two items of proposed legislation each account for a $300 million tax loss in 1974, liberalized deductions for individual pension plans, and a partial income tax credit for private elementary and secondary education. Although no details are presented in the budget, in the last Congress the Ways and Means Committee of the House acted favorably on a tax credit of approximately $200 per pupil for families of moderate and low income.

Corporate income tax receipts are projected at $37.0 billion in 1974, an increase of $3.5 billion over this year. The size of the increase reflects the rising share of corporate profits in gross national product that normally occurs during periods of rapid economic growth, such as is now being experienced.

Social insurance taxes and contributions—which have become the second largest source of federal revenue—are estimated to increase by $13.6 billion to a total of $78.2 billion in 1974. These figures reflect a recent important but in a sense unheralded tax increase—the rise in the combined employee-employer social security payroll tax rate from 10.4 percent to 11.7 percent effective January 1, 1973 and the rise in the taxable earnings base from $9,000 to $10,800 on January 1, 1973 and to $12,000 on January 1, 1974. An additional $600 million is estimated from proposed legislation to help finance recent increases in benefits under the railroad retirement system. For the fiscal year 1974, the various payroll tax revenues are estimated to be more than double the total proceeds of the corporate income tax and to equal 70 percent of the revenues from the personal income tax. This represents a dramatic shift from earlier years. A rising disenchantment with these social insurance "contributions" is now becoming visible even among some of the most staunch past supporters of social security programs.

Excise tax receipts in both 1973 and 1974 reflect the start of phasing out the telephone excise. This tax rate was reduced from 10 percent to 9 percent on January 1, 1973. Under present law, a further reduction to 8 percent is scheduled for January 1, 1974.

Tax reform. Aside from the modest recommendation for a credit for private school tuition, the 1974 budget does not contain any proposals to reform the federal tax structure. In February 1973, the House Committee on Ways and Means began an extensive set of hearings on a wide variety of potential changes in the revenue system. It is likely that considerable public attention will be devoted to the subject of tax reform as calendar 1973 unfolds.

Nevertheless, the complexity of tax legislation makes it unlikely that the House and the Senate will reach agreement on a tax reform bill this year. Tax reductions are often made retroactive but tax increases usually are made only prospectively. Thus, the revenue estimates presented in the new budget probably will not be subject to much if any change as a result of congressional action. Of course, during the extended congressional debates and public discussions, there could be significant repercussions on business expectations of the future—because many of the changes being suggested to the Congress involve increasing the tax burden on various forms of investment.

A subsequent chapter of this study presents a somewhat novel approach to one aspect of tax reform. It deals with the question of personal deductions on the federal income tax. The proposal presented there attempts to meet the concerns of tax reformers without eliminating the encouragement currently given to the support of private, voluntary solutions to national concerns.

Financing the deficit. The anticipated reduction in the unified budget deficit from $24.8 billion this year to $12.7 billion in fiscal 1974 has its counterpart in diminished requirements for federal borrowing from the public. Such financing is projected at $25.0 billion in fiscal 1973 and $16.5 billion in 1974. The decline in estimated borrowing is not as large as the improvement in the budget position primarily because $3.0 billion of this year's deficit is being covered by drawing down the Treasury's cash position; no net change in the cash balance is now being projected for next year.

Borrowing from the public has traditionally meant borrowing from domestic individuals and institutions. However, a significant change has occurred during the last few years. As shown in Table 19, the government's substantial borrowings during 1971 and 1972

Table 19
FEDERAL GOVERNMENT BORROWING FROM THE PUBLIC
(fiscal years, $ in billions)

	1968	1969	1970	1971	1972
Foreign and international	− 0.7	− 0.4	3.7	17.9	17.3
Domestic (excluding Federal Reserve System)	19.4	− 11.2	− 1.9	− 6.3	− 3.8
Total	18.7	− 11.6	1.9	11.6	13.5

(exclusive of Federal Reserve System operations) were accompanied by an actual decline in domestic holdings. Substantial sales were made to foreign and international accounts. Should the traditional pattern of domestic borrowing reassert itself, the smaller financing requirements in the coming year may turn out to have a stronger impact on domestic money markets than the larger financings of the past few years.

By the end of 1974, gross federal debt is expected to be $505.5 billion, with 72 percent held by the public (including the Federal Reserve System). The remaining 28 percent will be held by the departments and agencies, mainly the large social insurance trust funds. A total of 97 percent of the gross federal debt will have been issued by the Treasury and the remainder mainly by the Export-Import Bank, the Tennessee Valley Authority, and the Postal Service. Of the estimated $2.5 billion of federal agency borrowing from the public in 1974, more than half will be accounted for by the Export-Import Bank. Since August 17, 1971, that agency has been excluded from the budget proper but its rapidly growing volume of borrowings is included in federal borrowing from the public. This year, the newly enacted Environmental Financing Authority joins the list of special credit agencies. It will provide a "conduit" to the private credit markets for local governments who find it difficult to obtain the financing needed to meet federal waste treatment standards. Its transactions also are not included in the budget totals, but its borrowings are included in the figures on federal debt.

Despite the restraint on budget outlays per se, the activities of extrabudgetary credit agencies continue to expand. All of these agencies are essentially financial intermediaries, channeling funds from one sector of the capital markets to another. They borrow under federal auspices, in the "agency" sector of the bond markets, and lend these funds either directly or by purchasing loans originated by their special clientele. The net borrowing from the public by the government-sponsored enterprises (such as Fanny Mae, the federal land banks, and the home loan banks) is projected to rise from $7.7 billion this fiscal year to $9.5 billion next. The federal home loan banks and the relatively new Federal Home Loan Mortgage Corporation account for the great bulk of the rise. Also as indicated above, a new government-sponsored financial intermediary will start operation in 1974, the Student Loan Marketing Association; no estimates of its borrowing requirements are yet available. Legislation will again be requested to establish a federal financing bank to consolidate and improve the efficiency of financing federal agency obligations.

This would be a useful tool to deal with the growing proliferation of extra-budgetary federal credit programs.

The Problems Ahead

This year, for the first time, the federal budget presents a detailed preview of the next year's outlook. The estimates for the fiscal year 1975 show, on a full-employment budget basis, receipts of $290 billion and outlays of $288 billion. Thus—and this point is strongly emphasized in the Budget Message—if the expenditure restraint outlined by the President is achieved, the 1975 budget can show a $2 billion full-employment surplus without any tax increase.

As has been noted earlier in connection with the 1974 outlay estimates, there are a number of "ifs" that must be kept in sight. These restrained outlay figures can be achieved only if (1) the President and the Congress both refrain from major new spending initiatives, domestic and international, (2) the Congress provides the legislation necessary for certain program reductions, and (3) the agencies achieve the program economies and efficiencies promised in the new budget. Despite all the talk about program cutbacks, it is more realistic to expect a slowing down in the growth rate of public outlays.

A great sense of dissatisfaction with this fiscal policy is evident in the Congress. Yet, a widespread feeling of impotence seems to pervade the national legislature with reference to its ability to deal with the President in these matters. The Congress is struggling to develop a mechanism to enable it to exercise greater control over budgetary decisions, but thus far the effort is proving unsuccessful. The crucial problem is not that the executive has imposed its priorities on the budget. Rather, as a former congressional assistant has noted, "it is that Congress lacks a conclusive mechanism for asserting its own priorities in a budget of finite dimensions." [1]

In the short run, a standoff may be the best that càn be anticipated. The President can utilize his powers to effectuate significant reductions in government spending and modest reorganizations of the executive branch. But he is unlikely to obtain from the Congress the legislation necessary to achieve truly fundamental reforms. Similarly, the Congress seems unable to force the President to spend where he believes the objectives of government can be attained at lower costs, but it can and presumably will refrain from

---

[1] Alton Frye, "Mending the Frayed Congressional Pursestrings," *Washington Post*, December 23, 1972, p. A 18.

granting him legislative victories in the form of new Nixon initiatives. General revenue sharing may be the last major innovation in domestic policy for quite a while.

In the longer run, this deadlock is likely to be broken. One possibility is that a plethora of congressional investigations of executive branch activities and programs will weaken the President's position vis-à-vis the Congress. A more positive approach would be to strengthen the internal operations of the Congress so that forceful stands could be taken and followed through. Such resurgence of congressional power is likely to require more than expenditure ceilings and omnibus appropriation bills. Part II of this study is devoted to an analysis of the nature of the changes that would be required to improve the effectiveness of legislative decision making.

The intermediate-range outlook in the relationship between the Congress and the administration is for a period of continuing difficulties and unpleasantness. Such a situation would make ambitious new spending or tax initiatives less likely than in the past and, conversely, spending restraint more likely. Given the rapid expansion in economic activity and the concern over a rebirth of inflationary pressures, this budget outlook would seem to be consistent with the short-run needs of economic stabilization.

3

SHIFTING FROM INCOME TAX DEDUCTIONS TO CREDITS

The practice of permitting certain expenditures to be treated as deductions when calculating personal income tax has come under increasing attack. The basic criticism is that this practice is regressive. Because designated expenditures are treated as deductions from gross taxable income, the amount of the tax savings per dollar of designated expenditures depends on the tax bracket of the taxpayer. Thus an upper income taxpayer receives a larger tax reduction than does a lower income taxpayer for making the same dollar amount of charitable contribution—or payment for state and local taxes, mortgage interest or medical expenses, to name the other main "allowable" deductions.

In effect, the government subsidizes the taxpayer to the extent of 14 percent of allowable expenditures for those in the lowest tax bracket, 70 percent for those in the top bracket, and somewhere in between for others. (Those taxpayers claiming the standard deduction via the "short form" receive no subsidy for the expenditures they make in "allowable" categories.) To state the point in terms of an example, the subsidy for home ownership costs (real estate taxes and mortgage interest) becomes greater the more expensive the home and the larger the taxpayer's income. It should not be surprising that taxpayers in the upper and upper-middle tax brackets receive the bulk of the subsidy implicit in the present deduction system. As Table 20 shows, two-thirds of all the subsidies involved in the personal deduction system are received by taxpayers with adjusted gross income of $15,000 and over and 49 percent by taxpayers in the $20,000 and over category. In contrast, less than 15 percent of deductions are taken by taxpayers with adjusted gross income under $10,000.

Table 20

SUBSIDIES IMPLICIT IN PERSONAL DEDUCTIONS ON THE FEDERAL PERSONAL INCOME TAX

(calendar year 1971)

Adjusted Gross Income Class	Category of Personal Deduction ($ in millions)					
	State and local taxes	Chari- table contri- butions	Inter- est on home mort- gages	Consumer credit & misc. expenses	Medi- cal ex- penses	Total
$ 0 - 3,000	4	3	a	2	5	14
3 - 5,000	97	34	27	56	100	314
5 - 7,000	172	89	81	86	205	633
7 - 10,000	624	245	276	220	325	1,690
10 - 15,000	1,414	525	719	478	470	3,606
15 - 20,000	1,277	434	543	401	310	2,965
20 - 50,000	2,501	806	621	651	360	4,939
50 - 100,000	1,146	446	101	79	90	1,862
100,000 and over	1,065	893	32	22	35	2,047
Total	8,300	3,475	2,400	1,995	1,900	18,070

a Less than $500,000.

Note: An example might help the reader to interpret this table: If there had been no provision for the deduction of state and local taxes in 1971, individuals and families with adjusted gross income of less than $3,000 would have had to pay, in the aggregate, $4 million more in federal income taxes than they actually did pay that year.

Source: Computed from data of the U.S. Department of the Treasury.

This point is made implicitly by tax reformers when they advocate that all of these deductions from taxable income should be eliminated. But the proponents of this approach seem to reflect little, if at all, on the fundamental reasons for the deductions or on the consequences of their elimination.

The Rationale for Personal Deductions

Some personal deductions, one must readily admit, can hardly be defended and probably should be terminated. There has been no systematic review of the personal expenses allowable as deductions in calculating taxable income or of the consistency of such deductions with prevailing concepts of income or social policy.[1] For example,

---

[1] C. Harry Kahn, *Personal Deductions in the Federal Income Tax* (Princeton: Princeton University Press for the National Bureau of Economic Research, 1960), p. 12.

deductions of interest on consumer debt account for $1.8 billion, or 90 percent, of the "consumer credit and miscellaneous expenses" category of Table 1. It is hard to see why the general taxpayer should subsidize families that wish to go into debt to buy new refrigerators or second cars.

On the other hand, the largest category of deductions—far in excess of the others—is state and local taxes. This provision of the tax code furthers a clear objective of public policy: to strengthen state and local governments by offsetting in part the burden of the taxes they levy with a lower burden of federal taxes. This offset could be viewed as the original "revenue sharing" effort in our federal system. Moreover, in the absence of this deduction, some taxpayers could face a combined local, state and federal rate of income taxation close to 100 percent of income, bordering on sheer confiscation.

Charitable contributions are the second largest category of deductions. There are many reasons for such indirect public support of voluntary, private institutions. Such institutions provide diversity and free choice; they can experiment with different approaches to problems and enter fields too controversial for government agencies; and they often take on responsibilities that otherwise would have to be financed entirely by tax revenues.

The third largest category of deductible expenditures, interest on mortgages on owner-occupied homes, is designed to increase social stability by encouraging individual home ownership. The objective is furthered by the deductibility of residential property taxes, which account for almost a third of personal deductions for state and local tax payments (discussed above).

Some personal deductions are necessary refinements of gross income in order to arrive at a fair and equitable concept of a taxable income base. Cases in point are expenses related to the earning of income, such as those for union dues, child care for working wives, work clothing, and safe deposit boxes for securities.

Although most popular discussion of tax reform tends to ignore the substantive purposes of many of these allowable deductions, the underlying literature of public finance does not. In his definitive study of the subject, Professor C. Harry Kahn stated that personal tax deductions are designed to "differentiate between taxpayers whose incomes, though apparently equal, are of different sizes in some relevant sense."[2] Similarly, Professor Dan Throop Smith, who served as deputy to the secretary of the Treasury for tax policy at the time

---

[2] Ibid., p. 171.

of the adoption of the landmark Internal Revenue Code of 1954, claims that most, if not all, of the allowed deductions are intended to increase the fairness of the tax. As he puts it, "All of the deductions allowed in computing the taxable income of individuals are designed to give relief to the taxpayers benefitting from them and thereby [to] make the law fairer."[3] Thus, without prejudging their effectiveness, we should recognize that these special provisions, or at least most of them, are intended to promote what economists call horizontal equity: the equal treatment of equals. Professor Kahn goes on to state that the tax revenues foregone by permitting personal deductions should not be looked at simply as lost taxes. "If intended to spur private expenditures, for instance, in the philanthropic domain, the figures represent more accurately the tax cost to the government of encouraging expenditures which might otherwise have to be undertaken by government."[4]

Some of the more thoughtful proponents of tax reform are aware of these "side effects" of the special provisions that they would eliminate. When an alternative to allowable deductions is presented, it usually takes the form of a proposal for a federally financed program designed to accomplish the same or similar objectives. Such direct governmental spending seems to have many advantages: the public would have a clearer picture of the flow of federal spending; the Congress could exercise annual control over the size and distribution of these benefits; financial assistance to private individuals and groups benefitting from the program could be weighed against the desirability of government agencies' taking direct responsibility for the activities in question; and so on.

On reflection, however, the implications of moving from indirect to direct subsidization of private institutions are profound. In the literal sense, this move would mean putting private hospitals, orphanages, schools and similar social service and eleemosynary institutions into the federal budget. The opportunities for federal influence and control over the conduct of these private, voluntary organizations would be obvious and considerable. Moreover, the constitutional separation of church and state would probably prevent extending such direct financial support to church-related medical and educational facilities and certainly to the religious institutions themselves.

In many cases, indirect public support of these private-sector or state-local activities may be more economical than direct federal

---

[3] Dan Throop Smith, *Federal Tax Reform* (New York: McGraw-Hill Book Co., 1961), p. 90.

[4] Kahn, *Personal Deductions in the Federal Income Tax*, p. 171.

financing or operation. A rather clear example would seem to be nonprofit hospitals and schools for which the present indirect federal support—in the form of the inducement to private giving that the deduction provides—obviates the need for full government financing (and perhaps operation). Moreover, the diversity that results from a variety of public and private institutions reinforces an important characteristic of American society.

A Proposal for Change

Yet tax reform and other important objectives need not be in irreconcilable conflict. The mind of man should possess the ingenuity to develop a tax system that is more equitable for taxpayers while continuing to promote private and local efforts to deal with important problems. Deductions from taxable income do not constitute the only way of using the tax system to encourage a taxpayer to spend income in various desired directions. Their only obvious justification is the oldest one in bureaucracy: "It's the way we've always done it." The statement is literally accurate, because deductions have been part of the system since the income tax law was enacted in 1913.

A solution is at hand in the form of tax credits, already successfully used in some special areas. Although the distinction between allowable deductions and tax credits is usually considered a technicality exciting only to lawyers and accountants, the distinction is vital to our present concern.

Deductions are implicitly regressive, credits are not. In fact, credits are quite flexible from that point of view. For example, a tax credit of a fixed percentage of an expenditure has a progressive effect compared to the current system of deductions. In contrast, as pointed out above, the value of a deductible dollar varies with the taxpayer's bracket. Because of the progressive structure of the federal personal income tax, deductions provide proportionately larger benefits to taxpayers in upper brackets than to those in low or middle brackets.

Consider a tax credit equal to a percentage of allowable expenses, the percentage being the same regardless of income. With a 50 percent credit, for example, any taxpayer giving $200 to charity, whether in a higher or lower income bracket, would have his tax liability reduced by $100. Depending on the percentage credit, such a system would reinforce the progressivity of the personal income tax, since those whose marginal rates were below the percentage credit would have their average rates reduced, while the opposite would hold for those whose marginal rates were above the percentage credit.

The new tax treatment of contributions to political campaigns provides a precedent for the tax-credit approach. Beginning in 1972, a taxpayer may deduct such contributions up to a maximum of $50 from his or her taxable income ($100 in the case of married taxpayers filing a joint return). But alternatively, the taxpayer may credit half of such contributions against his or her tax liability, up to a maximum of $12.50 ($25 in the case of married taxpayers filing a joint return). Clearly, the credit alternative would provide an inducement for taxpayers in lower income brackets—similar to that provided taxpayers in higher brackets—to engage in this particular private activity.

It is interesting to note that numerous proposals have been made for substituting credits for specific categories of deductible expenses, such as charitable contributions.[5] However, these proposals have stopped short of recommending a general substitution of credits for deductions. Yet, the rationale offered for each specific substitution would seem to apply equally well to the general case. For example, the following justification of a tax credit for charitable contributions applies equally to private home ownership, privately financed medical care, et cetera: "The tax credit accords with the reasoning that an allowance for philanthropic contributions is a deliberate instrument of public policy to encourage decentralized decision making in the allocation and administration of funds in areas commanding the public interest."[6]

Types of Tax Credits

In the federal tax structure, tax credits are generally granted as a percentage of a specific item of income or outlay. Typical examples include partial or complete credits for retirement income, business investment, state inheritance taxes (as applied to federal estate taxes), taxes paid to foreign governments, state unemployment taxes paid by employers (as applied to federal unemployment insurance taxes), and the wages paid to employees hired under the work incentive program.

---

[5] For analyses of specific tax credit proposals, see Alan Pifer, "Revitalizing the Charitable Deduction," in Carnegie Corporation of New York, *Annual Report for the Fiscal Year Ended September 30, 1972*, pp. 3-12; Roger A. Freeman, *Income Tax Credits for Tuitions and Gifts in Nonpublic School Education* (Washington: American Enterprise Institute for Public Policy Research, 1972); Kahn, *Personal Deductions in the Federal Income Tax*, p. 89; Melvin I. White, "Deductions for Nonbusiness Expenses and an Economic Concept of Net Income," in U.S. Congress, Joint Economic Committee, *Federal Tax Policy for Economic Growth and Stability* (Washington: U.S. Government Printing Office, 1955), pp. 364-65.

[6] Kahn, *Personal Deductions in the Federal Income Tax*, p. 88.

The percentage to be used for a given tax credit would depend on how strong an incentive is deemed desirable in terms of public policy. Of course, the gain from creating an incentive would have to be weighed against the cost of raising lost revenue through some other means. Table 21 sheds some light on this question by showing the

Table 21
HYPOTHETICAL TAX CREDIT EQUIVALENT OF PERSONAL DEDUCTIONS
(data for calendar 1970)

Selected Personal Deductions	Total Amount Deducted ($ millions) (1)	Revenue Loss to Treasury ($ millions) (2)	Tax Credit Equivalent [a] (percent) (2)/(1)
Taxes paid	32,045	8,600	26.9
Interest paid	23,895	4,500	18.8
Contributions	12,918	3,750	29.0
Medical expense	10,588	1,700	16.0
Total	79,446	18,550	23.3

[a] These credits are equivalent only in an arithmetical sense. In fact, such credits at the same percentage for all income classes would stimulate expenditure habits quite different from those under the deduction system. This would be true because the percentage offset against marginal income tax rates would be higher for lower income classes and lower for higher ones than the present system.

Source: Internal Revenue Service, *Statistics of Income—1970 Individual Income Tax Returns*, Preliminary Report (Washington: U.S. Government Printing Office, 1972), p. 40; U.S. Treasury Department, *Effect of Selected Tax Provisions*, table prepared for Joint Economic Committee, May 22, 1971.

percentage tax credits which, if applied to 1970 income levels and outlay patterns, would have resulted in the same revenue loss to the Treasury as did the existing system of personal tax deductions. The major existing deductions average out to the equivalent of a 23 percent tax credit. There is, to be sure, an implicit and perhaps unrealistic assumption in this calculation that expenditures on deductible items would be the same under the tax credit proposal. Unfortunately, we cannot know how taxpayers would respond to the substitution because those in higher brackets would have a lesser incentive than at present and those in lower brackets a greater incentive.

In any event, the simple mechanism of a tax credit could play a major role in strengthening voluntary organizations in our society by making them more democratic. Because the proposed tax credit would operate to the overwhelming advantage of lower and moderate income taxpayers, it would create a vast new potential constituency for voluntary organizations, reducing the present dependence of those organizations on the wealthy few. It would also support other policy objectives, such as strengthening nonfederal institutions and the ability of families to finance their own homes and medical care.

Unlike the alternative of direct support through federal expenditure, substituting a tax credit for the existing system of personal deductions would move us further toward decentralizing decision making in our society and encouraging diversity in the way social objectives are achieved. It would encourage "voluntarism," while diminishing the "elitist" character of certain private organizations, particularly charitable ones.[7] It would help to reaffirm the nation's long-standing tradition of private and local initiative for the public good.

---

[7] Cf. Pifer, "Revitalizing the Charitable Deduction," and White, "Deductions for Nonbusiness Expenses and an Economic Concept of Net Income," pp. 364-66.

4
WAGE AND PRICE CONTROLS

The administration's fiscal policy, as revealed in the 1974 budget, has been discussed in earlier chapters. No consideration of government economic policy is complete, however, if it is focused solely on fiscal policy. Monetary policy and direct economic controls constitute two other extremely important instruments that the government can use to influence the economy.

Little is said in this report about monetary policy. There are basically two reasons for this. First, the monetary policy followed in 1972 has been surveyed elsewhere and no good purpose would be served by duplicating this work here.[1] Second, there is no clear and authoritative statement of the future course of monetary policy that compares with the statement of fiscal policy found in the budget.

Perhaps the only thing that can be said with reasonable assurance about monetary policy in 1973 is that there is little likelihood that it will be as expansionary as it was during 1972. In that year the money stock grew by more than 8 percent, a rate far in excess of its growth rate in any of the previous few years and high above its trend rate of growth during the 1960s. A move toward restraint in monetary policy, coupled with the "austere" fiscal policy outlined in the budget, might indicate that these traditional weapons were to bear the brunt of the battle for price stability in 1973 and that reliance on direct wage and price controls was to be lessened. The administration has indicated, however, that controls will be continued through 1973. The relative novelty of this weapon in the fight against inflation and its obvious

---

[1] See, for example, Phillip Cagan, "Controls, Monetary Policy and the Inflation, 1970-72" (Washington, D. C.: American Enterprise Institute, forthcoming), and Jerry L. Jordan, "Interest Rates and Monetary Growth," Federal Reserve Bank of St. Louis *Monthly Review* (January 1973), pp. 2-11.

importance dictate that it be discussed here. To appreciate the effects of controls, we must begin at the beginning with a discussion of the economic setting when they were introduced.

Prelude to Controls

The U.S. economy was in unusual straits in mid-1971: the unemployment rate was hovering in the neighborhood of 6 percent and showed no signs of falling very rapidly. Following the recession of the previous year, gross national product was growing, but at a painfully slow pace, and it would obviously fail to reach the 1971 target of $1,065 billion set for it by the Council of Economic Advisers. And while money wages were rising rapidly, it seemed inevitable to many observers that these wage increases would be eaten away by the continuing rise in the cost of living—as evidenced by the increase in the consumer price index of about 4½ percent during the previous 12 months.

All of these conditions seemed to indicate that the administration's original game plan was failing—or if not failing, at least working much too slowly. That game plan, it will be remembered, called for "hands off" the wage-price process, even to the extent of eschewing the use of "jawboning." When the administration came into office in 1969, its strategy was to rely on traditional monetary and fiscal policies to cool off an overheated economy, and thereby to reduce the rate of inflation. Once inflation was under control and inflationary expectations extinguished, these policies could then be used to stimulate the level of economic activity back up to a level consistent with a more acceptable rate of unemployment. The apparent failure of the 1969-70 recession to produce quick and noticeable improvements in the price and wage indices prompted many to doubt the efficacy of traditional stabilization tools. Arthur Burns, chairman of the Board of Governors of the Federal Reserve System, for example, suggested that the economy was not responding the way it had in the past and that the rules of the economic game had changed.

In hindsight, however, it is not so clear that the economy was reacting so very differently in 1970 and 1971 than it had in the 1950s and 1960s. The recession—which had been supposed to cure the inflation—was an extremely mild one by historical standards. The (seasonally adjusted) unemployment rate was never more than a tenth of a point above 6 percent even at the recession's low. And the recession lasted only from the last quarter of 1969 to the last quarter of 1970, with a decrease in "real" GNP of only slightly more than one-half of one percent, an insignificant amount.[2] By these standards, the 1969-70 recession was one of the mildest the economy had ever experienced. In contrast to the mildness of this recessionary "medicine," the inflationary ills to be cured were more severe than any the economy had experienced in the post-Korean War period. It would have been surprising if the rate of inflation had reacted more dramatically to the slowdown in the economy.

During and following the recession, however, some results in the fight against inflation did begin to appear. As is evident from Charts 1 and 2, the rate of inflation in consumer prices and in the general price level reached a peak during 1970 and then declined. This general pattern holds for other price indices as well, with one significant exception, the wholesale price index. As Chart 3 illustrates, there was no clearly discernible downward trend in wholesale prices. Since movements in the wholesale price index are widely interpreted to foreshadow movements in consumer prices, it is easy to understand how some observers could conclude that there is "no early price relief in sight"[3] and "[w]e're on the inflation rocket again. Inflation . . . is just beginning."[4]

Also indicative of a possible resurgence of inflation was the behavior of wages in the period immediately preceding the imposition of controls. Although unit labor costs peaked during 1970, as did most price indexes, compensation per manhour was rising at an average annual rate of 7.4 percent in the first half of 1971, as compared to an average annual rate of 7.1 percent in 1969-70 and 6.9 percent in 1968-69. And although average hourly earnings in contract construction were increasing at a slightly slower pace in the first half of 1971 than they had in the preceding two-year period (9 percent as compared to 9.5 percent), wages of other nonmanufacturing employees and of employees in manufacturing industries were rising substantially faster in the first half of 1971 than they had during the peak inflation years of 1969 and 1970. (The index for all employees rose from an average annual rate of 6.7 percent in 1969-70 to a rate of 7.7 percent in the first half of 1971.)[5] The absence of any strong downward trend in wages is illustrated in Chart 4.

---

[2] The statistical discrepancy in the 1970 GNP accounts was also in the neighborhood of one-half of one percent.

[3] *Business Week*, August 14, 1971, p. 21.

[4] George E. Smith, president of J. M. Tull Industries, cited in *Business Week*, August 7, 1971, p. 20.

[5] The earnings series is a fixed weight index, adjusted for changes in overtime in manufacturing and for interindustry shifts.

Chart 1
CONSUMER PRICE INDEX, ALL ITEMS, PERCENT CHANGE OVER SIX MONTH SPANS
(seasonally adjusted annual rate)

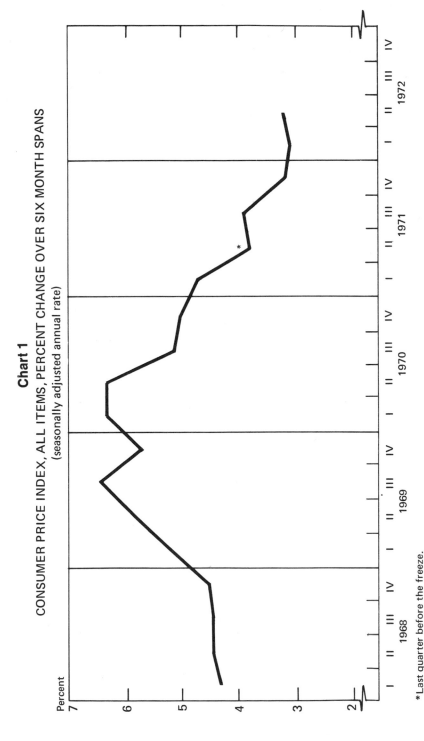

*Last quarter before the freeze.
Source: *Chartbook on Prices, Wages and Productivity*, January, 1973, U.S. Department of Labor, Bureau of Labor Statistics.

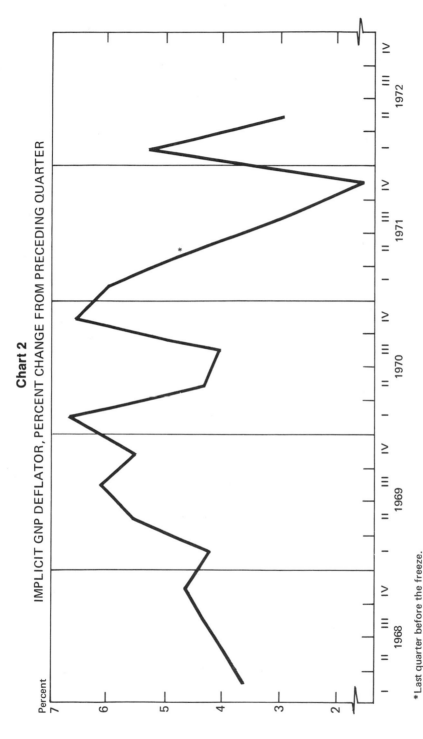

Chart 2

IMPLICIT GNP DEFLATOR, PERCENT CHANGE FROM PRECEDING QUARTER

*Last quarter before the freeze.
Source: *Chartbook on Prices, Wages and Productivity,* January, 1973, U.S. Department of Labor, Bureau of Labor Statistics.

55

Chart 3

CONSUMER PRICE INDEX, ALL ITEMS, PERCENT CHANGE OVER SIX MONTH SPANS

(seasonally adjusted annual rate)

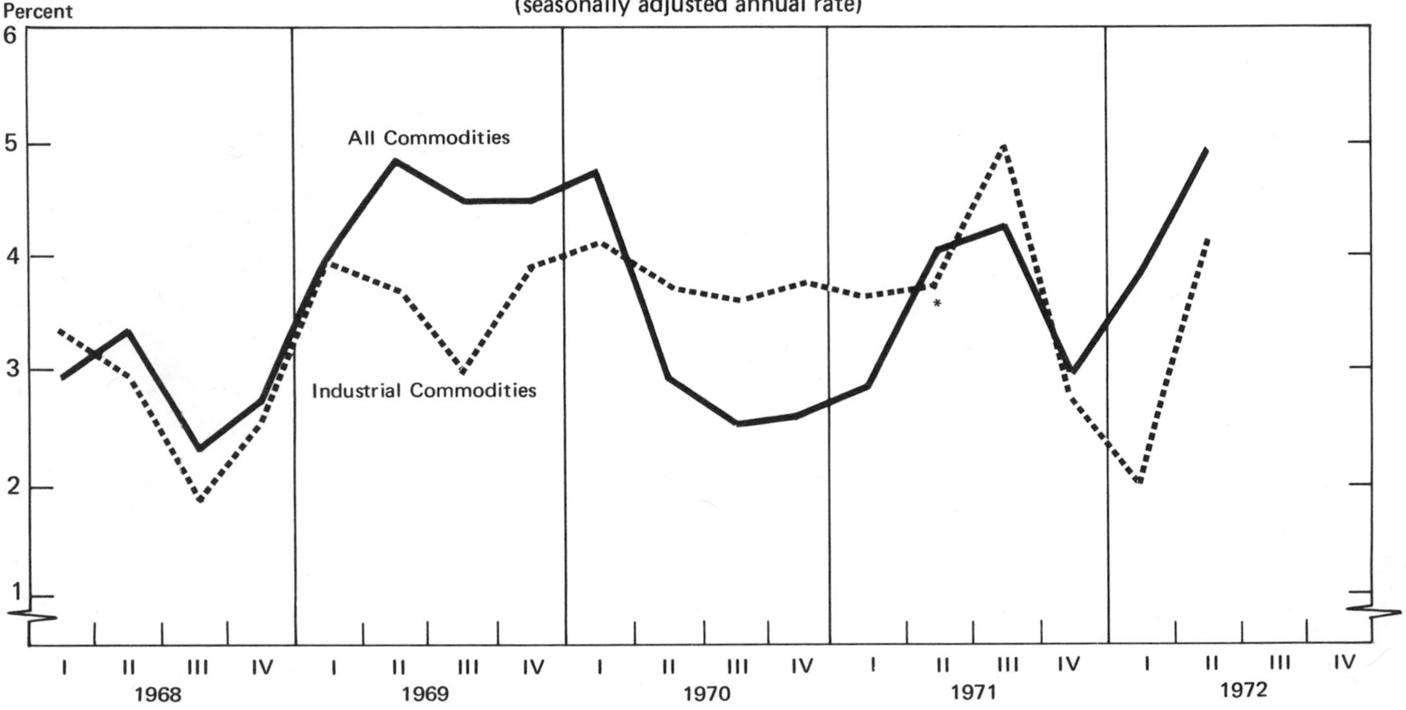

All Commodities

Industrial Commodities

Percent

6

5

4

3

2

1

I   II   III   IV   I   II   III   IV   I   II   III   IV   I   II   III   IV   I   II   III   IV
1968   1969   1970   1971   1972

*Last quarter before the freeze.

Source: *Chartbook on Prices, Wages and Productivity,* January, 1973, U.S. Department of Labor, Bureau of Labor Statistics.

56

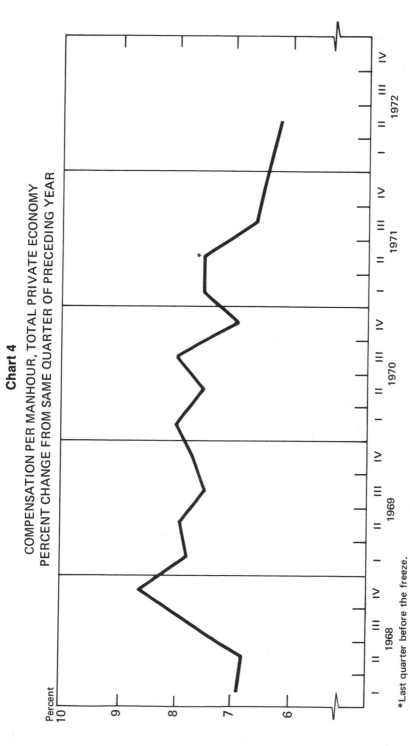

Chart 4

COMPENSATION PER MANHOUR, TOTAL PRIVATE ECONOMY
PERCENT CHANGE FROM SAME QUARTER OF PRECEDING YEAR

*Last quarter before the freeze.

Source: *Chartbook on Prices, Wages and Productivity,* January, 1973, U.S. Department of Labor, Bureau of Labor Statistics.

57

One other development which complicated the inflation picture in mid-1971 was that although the *trend* of prices had been downward, short-term movements had been generally upward. It was not known, of course, whether these upward movements represented aberrations from a trend that would continue its downward movement, or whether they signalled a reversal of that trend. While normally short-term movements might not be considered a signal of reversal, the situation in the middle of 1971 was such that this possibility was credible. For one thing, inflationary expectations had not been driven out of the system. And the federal budget for the fiscal year that began in mid-1971 had projected a deficit of almost $12 billion, which added to the fears of renewed inflation among many members of the economy. Another consideration that lent credence to the possibility that the increased rate of inflation during the spring of 1971 foreshadowed a reversal of the previous trend was that, in August 1971, the economy was in its ninth month of recovery from the recession. At that point in earlier recoveries, the rate of inflation had generally begun to accelerate rather than continue to decelerate.

The administration, then, was confronted with conflicting signals as to the future course of prices. Making the situation even worse was the forthcoming election, and the administration may well have felt that even improved price performance brought about by a hands off policy would be attacked as "not good enough," i.e., not as good as could have been achieved if an incomes policy had been adopted. Probably a combination of such political and economic considerations led to the adoption of an incomes policy in August 1971.

The Framework of Controls

The machinery of controls which was established during the 90-day freeze on prices, wages and rents is well-known and will be only briefly described. Overall responsibility for the stabilization program was vested in the Cost of Living Council (COLC). Wages and prices were under the jurisdictions of the Pay Board and the Price Commission, respectively. Rents, a particular type of price, were also controlled by the Price Commission, with the assistance of the Rent Advisory Board. Wages in the construction industry, which had been troublesome for some time and which had been brought under the responsibility of the Construction Industry Stabilization Committee in March 1971, remained under this committee; it became, formally at least, subject to the general standards and guidance of the Pay

Chart 5
ORGANIZATION OF THE ECONOMIC STABILIZATION PROGRAM IN 1972

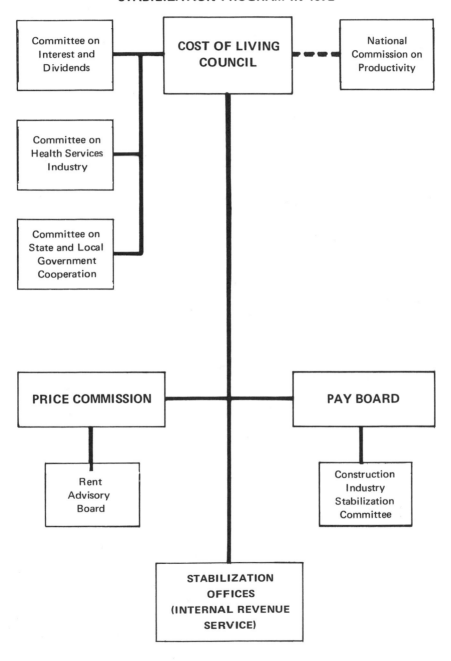

Board. The COLC was advised on problem areas by committees on interest and dividends, on health services, and on state and local cooperation. (See Chart 5.)

The Cost of Living Council was chaired by the secretary of the Treasury and was a cabinet level committee. The Pay Board was originally composed of 15 members drawn equally from business, labor and the general public. In March 1972, four of the five labor members withdrew in disagreement with a decision in the Pacific longshoremen's case. The board was then reconstituted to consist of seven "public" members, although one was a labor leader and one was a businessman. From the beginning, the Price Commission was composed of seven public members.

The original goal of the Price Commission was to reduce the rate of inflation to between 2 and 3 percent by the end of 1972. The Pay Board set an initial standard of limiting wage increases to 5½ percent per year. It revised the pay standard during 1972 to allow "catch-ups" for certain groups of workers, to exclude the "working poor" from controls, and to permit increased fringe benefits. (This latter revision raised the effective standard to 6.2 percent.) Price regulations were also modified during the year, the most important change being the elimination of certain sellers from the controllers' jurisdiction.

The price ceilings that were established permitted price increases in the same proportion as increases in allowable costs. (Generally increases in wages above 5.5 percent, even if approved by the Pay Board, were not "allowable" costs.) Also, wage increases were compared to normal productivity growth in order to determine the increases in unit labor costs that would be allowed to be passed through to higher prices. As a final check on prices, a price increase that would raise a firm's profit margin (i.e., profits as a percentage of sales) above the level in the best two of the three fiscal years preceding the freeze of August 1971 was not allowable.

Table 22 shows the classification scheme adopted to implement the control program. The largest firms and largest employee bargaining units were required to obtain advance approval for price and wage increases. Firms and bargaining units in the next largest group were required to report price and wage changes after the fact, but prenotification was not necessary. Controlled units in the third group were not required to obtain advance approval for price and wage changes nor to report such changes after they occurred; they were subject, however, to the standards of the control program and could be subjected to spot checks. A fourth group of firms and employee

Table 22
CLASSIFICATION OF FIRMS AND WORKERS IN ECONOMIC STABILIZATION PROGRAM [a]

Tier	Firm	Employees
I Prenotification of wage or price increases; quarterly reporting of price, sales, profits	Sales of $100 million and over (1,700 firms, 45 percent of sales)	Wage units of 5,000 or more workers (15 percent of total)
II Reporting of increases; quarterly reporting of price, sales, profits	Sales of $50 million to $100 million (1,700 firms, 5 percent of sales)	Wage units of 1,000 to 5,000 workers (6 percent of total)
III No reporting; subject to ESP regulations and monitoring	Sales of less than $50 million (1.5 million enterprises, 25 percent of sales)	Other workers (29 percent of total)

[a] As of the end of 1972 exemptions had been granted to 6.5 million enterprises with 25 percent of total sales and to 50 percent of all employees (including exempted employees of state and local governments).

Source: *Annual Report of the Council of Economic Advisers* (Washington: U.S. Government Printing Office, 1973), p. 152.

bargaining units was not subject to controls at all, and this group grew steadily during Phase II. By the end of 1972, 6.5 million enterprises (with 25 percent of total sales) and 50 percent of all employees (including exempted employees of state and local governments) were in the exempt category.

Effectiveness of Controls

A relatively simple and straightforward approach to evaluating the effect of the stabilization program on inflation is to compare the rates of increase in wages and prices prior to the imposition of the freeze with the rates of increase since that time.[6] During the controls period, the wholesale price index rose at virtually the same rate that it had during the first eight months of 1971. The consumer price index, however, rose at a substantially lower rate during the controls period (3.1 percent as compared to 4.8 percent). Price indexes with broader bases than either the CPI or the WPI show marked declines in the rate of inflation during the controls period. Thus the rate of increase

---

[6] Throughout this section all rates of growth, unless otherwise noted, are seasonally adjusted annual rates.

in the implicit GNP deflator during the control period, for example, was only about half of what it had been during the two quarters immediately preceding the imposition of controls (2.7 percent as compared with 5.1 percent). Other broad based indexes show decreases of roughly similar orders of magnitude (see Table 23).

Table 23
CHANGES IN SELECTED PRICE INDEXES IN PRECONTROL AND CONTROL PERIODS
(seasonally adjusted annual rates)

Price Index	Precontrol			Control
	Dec. '68 to Dec. '69	Dec. '69 to Dec. '70	Dec. '70 to Aug. '71	Aug. '71 to Dec. 72
Consumer Price Index	6.1	5.5	3.8	3.1
Wholesale Price Index	4.8	2.2	5.2	5.3
Implicit GNP deflator	5.3	5.3	5.1[b]	2.7[c]
Fixed weight GNP deflator[a]	5.4	5.1	5.9[b]	3.6[c]
Fixed weight personal consumption expenditures deflator[a]	5.0	4.3	4.5[b]	2.8[c]

[a] Implicit GNP deflators are affected by shifts in the composition of output; fixed weight deflators are not affected by these types of shifts.
[b] These figures are for the quarters 1970:IV to 1971:II.
[c] These figures are for the quarters 1971:II to 1972:IV.
Source: *Annual Report of the Council of Economic Advisers*, 1973, p. 57.

All of these indexes, of course, include some items which are not subject to price controls, such as raw agricultural products. If food prices are removed from the consumer price index to reflect the exemption just indicated, and if prices of used cars are removed to reflect the fact that prices of second hand goods are not controlled, and finally if mortgage interest rates are deleted from the index on the grounds that they are not directly controlled under the stabilization program,[7] the resulting index is a rough measure of the prices

---

[7] As noted in the previous section, interest rates are not controlled directly, although they are monitored by the Cost of Living Council's Advisory Committee on Interest and Dividends.

of goods which are controlled by the Price Commission. This adjusted index rose at an annual rate of 5 percent during the first eight months of 1971, but at only a 2.7 percent rate during the first year of controls.[8]

Wages show a similar, if less dramatic, improvement during the control period. Compensation per man-hour and average hourly earnings both increased at annual rates of about 6 percent under the controls, as compared to their respective average annual rates of growth of 7.4 and 7.7 percent during the first half of 1971.

These comparisons would seem to indicate that price controls have been much more effective than wage controls. One reason for this is that the "bulge" period immediately following the wage-price freeze had a much greater effect on wages than on prices. That is, some wage settlements negotiated prior to the freeze did not become effective until after the freeze, and some wage settlements which exceeded the guidelines established by the Pay Board were allowed to stand in order to reestablish long standing wage differentials.

If, in order to eliminate the effects of the freeze and "bulge" periods, the rate of increase in prices and wages prior to the control period is compared to the rate of increase in these variables during the second, third and fourth quarters of 1972 (i.e., a "representative" period of controls), the decreases in the rates of wage and price inflation become more nearly equal. As noted earlier, compensation per man-hour and average hourly earnings rose at annual rates of 7.4 and 7.7 percent, respectively, during the first half of 1971. In our "representative" control period, the compensation figure increased at an average annual rate of 5.7 percent while average hourly earnings rose at a rate of 5.6 percent per year. Table 24 compares prefreeze rates of increase in selected price and wage indexes with their rates of increase during the last three quarters of 1972.

This mixed bag of price performance, when compared to the 1.5 to 2 percentage point decrease in wage inflation during the "representative" period of controls, could easily lead one to the conclusion that wage controls have been more effective than price controls. The controls seem to have had some effect on both wages and prices, however, if comparisons of pre- and post-freeze rates of inflation are any indicator.

---

[8] Barry Bosworth, "Phase II: The U.S. Experiment with an Incomes Policy," *Brookings Papers on Economic Activity*, 1972: 2 (Washington: The Brookings Institution, 1972), p. 346.
The automobile excise tax, which was rescinded effective August 1971, has been deleted from the index for the precontrol period in order to make the two periods comparable.

Table 24

CHANGES IN SELECTED WAGE AND PRICE INDEXES IN PRECONTROL AND "REPRESENTATIVE" CONTROL PERIODS

(seasonally adjusted annual rates)

Index	Precontrol Period	Representative Control Period
Consumer price index	3.8	3.0
Wholesale price index	5.2	6.5
Implicit GNP deflator	5.1	2.3
Compensation per manhour	7.4	5.7
Average hourly earnings	7.7	5.6

Note: The precontrol period for the first two price indexes is from January to August 1971. The representative control period is from February to December 1972. For the wage indexes, and the GNP deflator, the precontrol period is the first two quarters of 1971; and the representative control period is the second third and fourth quarters of 1972.

Source: *Annual Report of the Council of Economic Advisers,* 1973, pp. 57, 60; Barry Bosworth, "Phase II: The U.S. Experiment with an Incomes Policy," *Brookings Papers on Economic Activity,* 1972:2 (Washington: The Brookings Institution, 1972), pp. 346, 348.

Just how well comparisons of pre- and post-freeze movements in prices and wages measure the effectiveness of the control program is debatable. Certainly the improvement in inflation is clear. But it is difficult to know how much of this improvement should be attributed to the control program because, as was noted above, inflation had begun to slow even before the initiation of the control program. This deceleration in inflation took place in response to market conditions that dictated less inflation. How much of the post-freeze deceleration in inflation is attributable to market conditions and how much to the controls cannot be answered by the straightforward approach of simply comparing pre- and post-freeze rates of inflation.

An approach to this question which can, in principle, distinguish between the effects of market forces and the effects of the controls on the rate of inflation is one which takes market forces explicitly into account. One way to do so is to compare forecasts of prices and wages made prior to August 1971—which were presumably based on predicted market conditions—with actual prices and wages after the imposition of the controls.

The consensus of economists surveyed by the American Statistical Association and the National Bureau of Economic Research in mid-1971 was that prices would increase at a rate of 4 percent over the four quarters beginning with the third quarter of 1971. This forecast was an upward revision of the 3.5 percent rate forecast earlier in 1971, and presumably reflected the poor behavior of the consumer price index in the second quarter of 1971. Deviating from this consensus forecast, the monetarist model of the economy developed and used by the Federal Reserve Bank of St. Louis, implied that the rate of inflation from the third quarter of 1971 to the second quarter of 1972 would be between 4.7 and 4.8 percent. Given the actual rate of inflation of 2.8 percent over this period, one might infer from the consensus forecast that controls reduced the rate of inflation by about 1.2 percentage points, and infer from the St. Louis Federal Reserve Bank forecast that controls had lowered the rate of inflation by about 2 percentage points.

Several difficulties are inherent in this approach to evaluating the effectiveness of the control program, however. First, of course, is the problem of choosing which forecast to compare the actual inflation rate to. Should one choose the consensus prediction, the St. Louis forecast, or some other estimate? Second, and more importantly, one could have more confidence in this approach to evaluating the controls if forecasters had a better record of accuracy. The method assumes that the forecast would have been accurate if the wage-price control program had not been inaugurated. This is certainly an act of faith, one that is difficult to justify in view of the poor performance of the forecasters over the previous two years. Former Commissioner of Labor Statistics Geoffrey H. Moore comments: "Throughout the period mid-1969 to mid-1971 the average of the forecasts surveyed each quarter put the increase in the GNP price deflator at about 3.5% for each four-quarter period ahead. The actual increases throughout this period were 5% or above." [9]

One reason that forecasts of price movements may be inaccurate is that forecasts of other variables in the economic system may be in error, and these errors may feed back into the price forecasts. A way of getting around this problem and still using the forecasting approach is to forecast prices and wages ex post, using the actual values of other variables in the economy, such as productivity, capacity utilization, unemployment, et cetera. The general procedure of ex post forecasting, or simulation, is to first specify a mathematical model of the relationships among the key economic variables of interest to the investigator. One equation in such a model, for instance, may specify changes in the price level (ΔP) as depending on the unemployment rate (U):

$$\text{Equation 1} \qquad \Delta P = a - bU.$$

[9] Geoffrey H. Moore, Letter to the Editor, *Wall Street Journal*, August 8, 1972.

Statistical techniques are then employed to ascertain the average relationship between these two variables over some sample time period, such as from the beginning of 1955 through the first half of 1971. This relationship might be:

$$\text{Equation 2} \qquad \triangle P = .05 - 1.8 \, U,$$

indicating that, on average during the sample period, an increase of one unit in the unemployment rate was associated with a decrease of 1.8 units in the rate of increase in prices.

The final step in ex post forecasting is to insert values of U from the post-sample period, say the period of controls, into equation 2 and to solve the equation for the value of $\triangle P$. This value of $\triangle P$ indicates what the change in the price level would have been if the average relationship that existed during the sample period continued to exist during the post-sample period. This estimate can then be compared to the actual level of prices during the post-sample period to determine the effectiveness of the price control program.

The ex post forecasting approach has been employed by the Price Commission, by Professor Robert J. Gordon and by the author of this analysis. The models used in these investigations, of course, were much more complex than the illustrative model shown above as equation 1. Professor Gordon's model, for example, makes the change in the price level depend on four variables and the growth in average hourly earnings depend on seven variables (including three different measures of labor market tightness).[10]

The Price Commission's study indicates that if there had been no controls, inflation would have been 1.5 percentage points higher than it actually was. The model found no significant effect of the controls on wages.[11] Gordon estimated that if there had been no controls, prices would have increased 1.85 percentage points faster than they actually did, and wages would have increased by an additional 0.68 percentage point.[12]

The author examined the wage and price sector of a condensed version of the Wharton econometric model and found that the GNP deflator would have risen about 1.6 percentage points faster, at an annual rate, if there had been no controls. The model implies

---

[10] Robert J. Gordon, "Wage-Price Controls and the Shifting Phillips Curve." *Brookings Papers on Economic Activity*, 1972: 2 (Washington: The Brookings Institution, 1972), pp. 398-99, 407.

[11] The Price Commission's study has not been made public. The conclusions reported above are based on a speech by commission member Robert Lanzilotti at Georgetown University's annual Banker's Forum, September 29, 1972.

[12] Gordon, "Wage-Price Controls and the Shifting Phillips Curve," pp. 385-421.

that compensation per man-hour would also have risen at about the same faster rate.[13] The absolute difference found between the forecasted and actual rates of increase in wages and prices is about the same, 2 percentage points. But this difference represents a much larger relative reduction in prices—on the order of 40 percent—than in wages—on the order of 25 percent.

Ex post forecasting is probably the most sophisticated of the three techniques that have been discussed. This is not to say, however, that there are no problems with this approach. One obvious problem relates to the choice of the mathematical model relating prices and wages to other variables in the economy. If the model is mis-specified —if, for example, prices and wages are actually determined by variables not included in the model—then the model will not necessarily give good estimates of wages and prices. The choice depends primarily on a priori considerations, specifically, on the theory of price determination that a particular investigator accepts. Since there are many theories of price determination, there are many ways to decide which model of wages and prices is preferable. This is one of the reasons why the results of several models, all based on somewhat different theories of the price and wage determination process, are presented in this chapter.

An indication of the usefulness of the ex post forecasts can be gained by comparing forecasted and actual inflation for time periods subsequent to the development of the model but prior to the imposition of controls. The Gordon model, for example, was designed and "fitted" over the period ending with the fourth quarter of 1970. Forecasts of prices for the first two quarters of 1971, a period after the model was constructed but prior to the imposition of controls, can be compared with actual inflation in those two quarters to provide some information about the reliability of the estimates. The Gordon model predicted inflation (in the fixed weight private nonfarm deflator) at an annual rate of 3.91 percent during the first half of 1971. The actual rate of increase was 4.65.

This result can be interpreted in two ways. First, one might conclude that the model has a tendency to underpredict price changes.

---

[13] The basic model was taken from E. Phillip Howry, "Dynamic Properties of the Wharton Model," in Bert G. Hickman, ed., *Econometric Models of Cyclical Behavior* (New York: Columbia University Press, 1972). Reduced form equations for the GNP deflator, the personal consumption deflator and compensation per man-hour were estimated over the period 1953:I to 1971:II. The reduced form approach was used to get around the simultaneous determination of wages and prices. See Kenneth F. Wallis, "Wages, Prices and Incomes Policies: Some Comments," *Economica*, August 1971, pp. 304-10.

This would imply that the estimate of the effectiveness of controls should also be interpreted as an underestimate. Second, it could be argued that two quarters is too short a period to learn anything about the model's general tendency to over- or underestimate, and that the only permissible conclusion is that the model does not forecast well, period. Under this interpretation, the estimate of the effectiveness of the controls should be disregarded.

Another rather technical problem with the ex post forecasting approach results from the fact that most economic variables are related to their own values in earlier periods. This is hardly surprising; it simply means that if inflation is high in the current quarter, it will probably be high in the next quarter. But this characteristic of the data causes problems for the statistical technique used to estimate the average relationship between wages and prices and the explanatory variables over the sample period. In particular, the estimated relationship will be unreliable when "autocorrelation," as described above, is present. This problem reduces the significance one can attach to estimates of the effectiveness of the control program.

A discussion of the effectiveness of the control experiment would not be complete without some mention of the effect of controls on inflationary expectations. It is generally believed that an inflationary psychology developed during the late sixties and carried over into the seventies. This attitude was supposed to have made labor more insistent on large wage increases so that it could keep ahead of, or at least abreast of, rising prices. The same psychology is said to have made business less reluctant to grant large wage increases since it was expected that those increases could be passed forward in the form of higher prices, and would not diminish profits.

Some analysts, notably those who take a dim view of attempting to evaluate the effectiveness of the controls by comparing actual and predicted price and wage behavior or by comparing pre- and post-freeze developments, suggest that controls reduced inflationary expectations, and thereby reduced the rate of inflation. This explanation is not inconsistent with the approaches mentioned above, of course, but it does not rely on them.

It seems that controls did indeed reduce inflationary expectations. Direct support for this thesis comes from the diffusion index of inflationary expectations published by the Bureau of Labor Statistics.[14] The survey taken after the imposition of controls revealed a sharp

---

[14] Bureau of Labor Statistics, "Chartbook on Prices, Wages, and Productivity." Expectations of course are not directly observable. The BLS series presents a diffusion index of expected future prices. See the chartbook for an explanation.

downward adjustment of expectations.[15] A difficulty with the use of diffusion indexes to measure inflationary expectations is that these indexes reveal only the fraction of respondents who expect prices to rise. They do not indicate how strongly these expectations are held or, more importantly, how large a rise in prices is expected. Assume, for example, that in one period 70 percent of the respondents indicate that they expect prices to rise and that, although they do not indicate this in the survey, they expect prices to rise on average 3 percent. In the next period, assume that only 60 percent of the respondents indicate that they expect prices to rise in the future, but they think prices will rise by 10 percent. It is not at all clear that we should conclude from this that inflationary expectations have decreased.

Other evidence supporting the proposition that controls reduced inflationary expectations is to be found in the behavior of interest rates following the announcement of the freeze. Interest rates are determined by a multitude of forces, one of which is expected inflation. If inflation is expected to increase, lenders will add an "inflation premium" on top of the interest rate they would otherwise have charged, producing a higher interest rate. Similarly, if inflation is expected to decrease, the inflation premium can be reduced or removed, resulting in a lower interest rate. Immediately following the announcement of the freeze on August 15, 1971, the yield on seasoned three- to five-year U.S. Treasury securities fell 40 basis points (100 basis points equal 1 percentage point). And Moody's index of the yield on Aaa long-term bonds fell 20 basis points.[16] These decreases are difficult to interpret as anything except a reflection of expectations of reduced inflation.

The problem with this analysis of inflationary expectations is that one does not know if these expectations were permanently reduced by the imposition of controls, or whether the reduction was only a temporary reaction that was later reversed. Interest rates did rise subsequently. Was this because inflationary expectations had been revised upward, or did it simply reflect more basic structural forces, such as the demand and supply of credit?

In summary, we have looked at several ways to evaluate the effectiveness of controls—by comparing precontrol inflation with inflation under controls, by comparing predicted inflation with actual inflation, and by considering the effect of controls on inflationary

---

[15] It is assumed in the text that the survey which measured expectations in the fourth quarter of 1971 was the first such survey to be made following the announcement of the freeze.

[16] *Annual Report of the Council of Economic Advisers*, p. 64.

expectations. Each of these approaches has serious inherent short-comings. But *all three approaches imply that controls reduced the rate of increase in the price level,* although the amount of this reduction is not agreed upon. And *most of the approaches find that controls slowed the rate of increase in wages.* Two reactions are possible. First, the "purist" position would be to disregard these findings because of the shortcomings of the techniques. Second, the "practical" position would be to accept the presumption of the effectiveness of the controls—in other words, place the burden of proof on those who argue that the controls have had no effect. The reader is, of course, free to choose for himself between these two positions. It may be worthwhile, however, for the author to indicate his own, tentative, conclusion.

Evidence on the effectiveness of controls obtained by comparing pre- and post-freeze prices or by comparing actual and predicted inflation is unconvincing. In the first method, the implicit denial of the role of market forces is untenable. In the second, too large a "leap of faith" is required, given the poor record of price forecasts prior to the imposition of the freeze.

The freeze probably did have some, perhaps slight, positive effect by reducing inflationary expectations. Evidence to support this conclusion has already been presented. Notwithstanding the difficulties of gauging expectations, the behavior of interest rates and the index of price expectations do give us some reason to believe that expectations were revised downward after the freeze was announced. While they may have risen somewhat subsequently, it is doubtful that they ever reached the high level that obtained immediately prior to the freeze.

If the only benefit of the control program was the modification of expectations upon the announcement of the freeze, the question of the usefulness of Phase II is raised. It is suggested here that what Phase II did, with all its regulations, was to limit the upward revision of expectation following the freeze to a level below what would have been reached if there had been no follow-up to the freeze.

The Costs of Controls

Economic controls impose several types of costs on the economy. These costs, as well as the benefits of a lower rate of inflation, must be considered in evaluating the control program as a whole.

One type of cost involves the administrative costs of the control program. In this respect, the freeze and Phase II compare most favorably with other control episodes. While the administration of price controls occupied 60,000 people during World War II, and about 15,000 during the Korean War, only about 4,000 people (including about 3,000 from the Internal Revenue Service) were employed in administering the price and wage controls during 1972. And administrative expenditures for Phase II amounted to only about $80 million. To these figures, of course, it is necessary to add the manpower and money spent by firms and labor organizations in filing applications, keeping the required records, legal fees, et cetera. No estimate is available of the magnitude of this cost, but it is surely substantial.

Another, potentially more important, type of cost is the real cost of inequities, shortages and inefficiencies, all of which are frequently associated with attempts to restrain wages and prices. Inequities certainly arose under the freeze and Phase II. Price Commission and Pay Board regulations were formulated in very broad language, and some individual firms and labor bargaining units were caught in undesirable positions. Removal of inequities was slow.

On a larger scale, inequities are sometimes taken to refer to the distribution of income between large classes, such as wages and profits. There is little evidence that the controls affected this distribution very much. Labor's share of the output of the economy, measured in any one of a number of ways, remained relatively constant during the control period, despite the fact that output was rising rapidly. In the past rapidly rising output has been associated with declines in labor's share.

A full-scale study of the effect of Phase II on the availability of particular goods and on the efficiency of the production process has not yet been made. Preliminary indications are, however, that these effects were not very important. The shortages frequently associated with price controls are generally caused by excess demand and rigid price ceilings. Excess demand was not a general problem during 1972, however, and the administration of the control program was sufficiently flexible so that price ceilings did not cause very serious distortions. Shortages did arise in some areas to be sure. Timber and gasoline are perhaps the most frequently cited cases where controls seem to have had some distorting effect. In general, however, distortions of this type were almost nonexistent.

Use of the cost-plus type of price control adopted by the Price Commission inevitably creates some incentive to inefficiency. If a firm sees that its profits are going to exceed the profit margin ceiling, for example, it may provide added perquisites for its executives such as chauffer-driven limousines, thereby increasing its costs and reducing its profits. The Price Commission has kept a close watch for such developments, but has found none. One possible reason is that not many firms had reached their profit ceilings during 1972. In any event, the Council of Economic Advisers reported that, for 1972, "even anecdotal evidence of antiproductivity effects is rare." [17]

The Future of Controls

On January 11, 1973, the President announced Phase III of his economic stabilization program. The wage and price control standards of Phase II were retained, but compliance was made voluntary for all of the economy except for three particularly troublesome sectors: food processing and wholesaling, health care, and construction.

It is easy to exaggerate the difference between Phase II and Phase III, but how much has really changed? Firms are still constrained by a profit margin rule in setting prices. Labor is still expected to abide by a 5.5 percent pay standard. Compliance of both business and labor is nominally voluntary, but the administration retains the power (the celebrated "club in the closet") to force rollbacks in both prices and wages if its standards are violated. Finally, much of the compliance with Phase II regulations was voluntary—a fact not widely appreciated. By the end of 1972, 8 million enterprises with 50 percent of total sales were either exempt from price controls or were subject to only spot checks by the controllers. The comparable figures for labor are even more striking: by year-end 1972, 79 percent of all labor was either exempt from controls or subject to only spot checks.

But just as it is easy to exaggerate the difference between Phase II and Phase III, so it is easy to exaggerate their similarity. Phase III must surely be interpreted as a relaxation, and perhaps as a prelude to the end, of controls. The base period for calculating profit margin ceilings has been lengthened, permitting higher ceilings. Prenotification requirements, except in the food and health sectors, have been abandoned. Only about 800 firms are required to file quarterly reports of price changes and profit margins; only employee units of 5,000 or more must file reports on wage changes.

There is one other important difference between Phase II and Phase III. The latter has a "lower profile": fewer reports will be filed, fewer administrating agencies will be involved, fewer press releases will be distributed. This is the most important change in the control machinery. Why? What is the advantage of the controllers' being

---

[17] *Annual Report of the Council of Economic Advisers*, 1973, p. 67.

less visible? The key advantage is that they can disappear more quietly.

In 1972, controls had an almost ideal environment in which to operate. For one thing, the contract negotiations calendar was very light, with only 2.8 million workers affected by major bargaining negotiations that year. Growth in national income, although rapid, did not press against the limits of the economy's ability to produce: manufacturing capacity utilization rates were below 80 percent for the year, and unemployment averaged about 5.5 percent. In 1973, in contrast, more than 4.5 million workers will be affected by major collective bargaining negotiations. Moreover, capacity utilization rates are already reaching very high levels in some sectors, and unemployment (especially among the most sought after types of labor) should decline to, and perhaps below, the rate that is consistent with price stability.[18]

All of these factors tending to produce renewed inflation will be reflected in wage demands. Inflationary expectations will probably resurface during the course of the year as a result, and they will be strengthened by the increases in food prices that are all but unavoidable, at least through the first half of the year.[19]

Phase II regulations were not designed to cope with this sort of demand-pull inflation, and neither are the looser controls of Phase III. It has been suggested that rather than see the control machinery destroyed by the forces of demand-pull inflation, the administration has decided to simply let the controls fade away, as did the wage-price guidelines of the Kennedy and Johnson administrations. The "club in the closet" may be used in the early part of the year if the administration thinks that cost-push is the villain. However, as the year wears on and demand-pull rears its head, it is reasonable to expect that the club will be taken out of the closet less and less frequently, until it is not taken out at all.

---

[18] In November 1972, the unemployment rate for married males over the age of twenty stood at 2.1 percent, about as low as it can go without endangering price stability. For the importance of "specific" unemployment rates, see William Fellner, *Employment Policy at the Crossroads: An Interim Look at the Pressures to be Resisted* (Washington, D. C.: American Enterprise Institute, 1972).

[19] It should be noted that many observers feel that inflationary expectations have already resurfaced. In support of this thesis, they point to the decline in the stock market during the first two months of the year and the flight from the dollar which led to devaluation in mid-February.

Part Two:
Reforming the Budget Process

5
DEVELOPMENT OF THE APPROPRIATIONS PROCESS

Money, according to Alexander Hamilton, is the vital principle of the body politic. How it will be spent and who controls it are enduring issues sure to produce strong and conflicting opinions. Such issues are the substance of the politics of the budget process; their resolution shapes party and institutional fortunes.

Congressional action on the budget for fiscal year 1973 shows the extent to which fiscal policy can be captive of the budget process. The President's 1972 request that Congress pass a spending ceiling bill as an anti-inflationary measure, implied an indictment of Congress's control of the budget and of congressional budget procedures. Its use of the power of the purse challenged, Congress is confronted with a controversy far deeper than the routine, though sometimes heated, debates over particular programs or particular budget items.

Congress must face this challenge, for it flows from laws, such as the 1946 Employment Act, directing the President to oversee the nation's economic well-being. According to law and precedent, the President's judgment as to the budget's fiscal and program impact must be put into suggestions for legislative action. But the Constitution expressly gives Congress the right to control the power of the purse. If the budget is "out of control," the practical questions are why, who will take control of it, and what kind of budget process should Congress use to control public funds.

The history of the appropriations process sheds light on the far-reaching implications of these questions. That history is reviewed here as a foundation for the budget reform proposals presented in Chapter 6.

The Formative Period

From the first attempts to organize the financial operations of the federal government, the appropriations process has evolved to keep pace with political necessity. The nation's first budget crisis, which occurred as Washington's administration drew to a close, contained much the same mix of variables as the present one. The great question then was the role of fiscal policy itself.

The earliest congresses struggled to fulfill the proud claim of *The Federalist* papers that there was a "new science of politics." Practical matters of public finance were especially hard to reconcile with the requirement that laws duly enacted by elected representatives were to be faithfully applied. This was to be "a government of laws, not men." To avoid the weaknesses of the Confederation, the Founding Fathers gave the new national institutions the powers thought necessary to preserve a union. But no guarantee can be fashioned to ensure that powers bestowed are exercised fully or beneficently. "Auxiliary precautions" were expected to supplement the constitutional safeguards. Divided control over the exercise of the power of the purse is one such precaution.

Fundamental guidelines were laid down in the Constitution for the control of government expenditures.[1] First, "no money shall be drawn from the treasury, but in consequence of appropriations made by law" (Article I, section 9). Second, since "all bills for raising money shall originate in the House of Representatives" (Article I, section 7), this body was to be the centerpiece of expenditure control. This special position was given the House of Representatives because, as the more popular and frequently elected of the two houses of Congress, it represented more directly those who would bear the brunt of the expenses of government. If its actions were too lavish, too frugal, or unfair, the Senate and the President could obstruct or refine them. Also, a remedy was always available at the next election.

The Treasury Act of 1789, passed by the "second constitutional convention," provided for executive initiative in the overall framing of financial policy as a means for Congress to exercise its power of the purse effectively. This act instructed the secretary of the Treasury to prepare estimates of spending and revenues and to submit financial reports to Congress.

The practical problems of public finance, problems beyond those of establishing the constitutional and legal guidelines, quickly become

---

[1] Joseph Story, *Commentaries on the Constitution of the United States* (Reprint of 1833 ed., New York: Da Capo Press, 1970), vol. II, pp. 366-502.

objects of political controversy. Honoring old debts, encouraging commercial interests, acquiring state property, the new financial policies of the national government—matters such as these were the issues. Grave political questions arose as the transition period ended: what are the limits of government action and the proper objects of government concern? General agreement that union was preferable to confederation was replaced with disagreement over particular policies.

In these early years, budget policy was decided in the Committee of the Whole House on the State of the Union. This procedure squared with the general view that Congress should act only after full deliberation. However, the procedure also inclined Congress to accept the leadership of the executive. Accounts of the financial policies established by early Congresses attest to the initiative and influence exercised by the various secretaries of the Treasury. Critics of strong centralized government feared that the executive would gain ascendance over Congress by means of dominating financial actions and that this would be a first step toward undermining the foundations of self-government.

The Jeffersonian party (soon to be called Republican), believing in a vigorous exercise of Congress's prerogatives, supported the Committee of the Whole procedure. An open Congress would encourage all members to speak, participate, and decide. Even more important, it would tend to encourage deliberation and to discourage partisanship. Jefferson described the position and the procedure of the Committee of the Whole in his *Manual of Parliamentary Procedure.*

> Matters of great concernment are usually referred to a committee of the Whole House, where general principles are digested in the form of resolutions, which are debated and amended until they get into the shape which meets the approbation of a majority. These being reported and confirmed by the House and then referred to one or more select Committees. . . .[2]

It was impossible to handle all congressional business in this way, because details could not be assigned to agents of the House—that is, select, or later, standing committees—until after the majority's will was known. When the Republicans gained control first of the Congress (1796) and then of the presidency as well (1800), they had to discover an agent of the "Whole House" to which items of detail

---

[2] Lewis Deschler, *Jefferson's Manual and Rules of the House of Representatives,* (Washington: U.S. Government Printing Office, 1961), p. 143.

could be referred for study and deliberation free from executive influence. They found such an agent in select legislative committees.[3]

There were difficulties, however, in this solution of vesting Congress's power in the Committee of the Whole while relying on committees for the detailed work necessary to legislative action. The Republicans' desire for a strong and independent Congress was frustrated by the press of daily business. If Congress insisted on meeting regularly in Committee of the Whole in order to avoid alienating any of its power to selected members, then it could not prepare the legislation that would make it independent. Some specialization and division of labor was necessary if there was to be a vigorous Congress. Faced with a choice between two conflicting goals, Congress favored the more important and gradually, through changes in its internal organization, remade itself into a major lawmaking body. Creation of a congressionally dominated appropriations process was the linch-pin of this strategy.

The Committee on Ways and Means of the House of Representatives was used by the Republicans in Congress as early as 1796 to question the government's policies. After 1800 this committee gradually assumed more responsibility for the initiation and formulation of financial policy, although, for a time, final action by Congress was preceded by general discussion in the Committee of the Whole House. However, the principles that were to guide Ways and Means when it formulated policies slowly came within its scope. By the 20th Congress financial questions went to the Whole House in theory only; in practice the Committee on Ways and Means made the recommendations and provided the detailed study.[4]

Types of Appropriations Processes

Congress has experimented with three kinds of appropriations processes, the Congressional, the National, and the Executive. The Congressional appropriations process coincided with the rise of the Republican-Democratic party originally led by Jefferson and Jackson and it lasted until 1860. The National appropriations process coincided with the emergence of Lincoln's Republican party at the beginning of the Civil War and continued almost until the rise of a new

---

[3] George B. Galloway, *History of the United States House of Representatives*, 87th Congress, 1st session, House Document No. 246 (Washington: U.S. Government Printing Office, 1962).

[4] Joseph Cooper, "Jeffersonian Attitudes Toward Executive Leadership and Committee Development in the House of Representatives," *The Western Political Quarterly*, March 1965, pp. 45-63.

Democratic party in 1936. The Executive appropriations process, which is the current type, actually antedated the administration of President Franklin D. Roosevelt, but it anticipated presidential leadership.

The Congressional appropriations process. Disagreements about the wisdom of Federalist financial policies were resolved with the development of a formal appropriations process. In 1802, in order to restrict the latitude of the executive, Congress empowered the Committee on Ways and Means to compel a detailed accounting of expenditures from the executive. Strengthened organization within Congress was the first step toward freedom from executive influence.

President Jefferson used informal party mechanisms (weakening the formal powers of the presidential office by giving greater control over public policy to Congress's majority) in a move calculated to benefit the Republican-Democratic party over the long term. The majority party, guided by party leaders, was to decide how the power of the purse was to be used.[5] An appropriations process substantively directed by the congressional majority would prevent general control of federal funds by the chief executive.

The new appropriations machinery was weighted against the active national policies sought by the Federalists and in favor of decentralization and central government restraint. Policies of the latter kind increased the advantages of the "agrarian" supporters of the Republican-Democratic party. With the center of political gravity firmly fixed in the congressional constituency, the defeated Federalist party collapsed and disappeared. Its successor, the Whigs, failed to move the federal government toward national programs. Even in those years when the Whigs controlled Congress, they broke ranks against balky Presidents who refused to do their bidding. What made the Whig defeat ironic was the discretionary power remaining in the presidency to expend and impound appropriated funds with near impunity.

A key feature of the Congressional appropriations process was the exercise of the two fundamental functions, taxation and expenditure, by a single committee, Ways and Means. As the Civil War approached, this committee was the most powerful body in Congress. Another feature of the process, flowing from the Democratic party's faith in limited government and its opposition to commercial interests was that revenue policy was more important in determining the out-

---

[5] William S. Chambers, *Political Parties in a New Nation* (New York: Oxford University Press, 1963).

comes of the appropriations process than spending policy. The one initiative allowed the executive throughout this period was an active program of debt retirement to preserve the national government's public credit. In this special sense, the Congressional type of appropriations process followed Hamilton's design: overall budget limits were established by the President through his reckoning of the revenue needed to preserve public credit. When the revenue needed for debt retirement was decided upon, Congress allocated the remainder as it saw fit. The remainder was always insufficient to fund anything more than minimum functions—government operations, foreign affairs, and national security.

The distinguishing marks of this appropriations process were the coupling of expenditure and taxation at the heart of the process and the influence of revenue levels in shaping policy. Congress filled out the system by creating numerous expenditure committees (forerunners of the present Government Operations Committees) to investigate the use and implementation of appropriations as new government agencies were created. While it was consistent to complement restricted government programs with detailed inquiry into the use of funds, such consistency led to practical absurdities. Elaborate congressional attempts to control funds by writing ever more specific appropriations laws prompted innovative efforts by the executive to preserve its discretionary control over the use of funds. Despite Congress's attempts, opportunities for discretionary spending by the executive abounded. The result was the opposite of that intended: in practice, Congress's control over the expenditure of federal funds was as lax as its appropriations measures were specific.[6]

The problems came to a head when Congress, as an antidote to overly specific appropriations, granted the executive powers to transfer funds among programs and carry forward unspent appropriations into the next year. This precipitated chaos, with appropriations and expenditures completely out of phase. But the Congressional type of appropriations process lasted a while longer because Presidents tended to refrain from using discretionary executive power to infringe upon any of the basic issues dear to the Democratic party—states' rights, agrarianism, free land, and cheap money.

The National appropriations process. The Civil War settled a number of fundamental issues, and the Democratic party was one of the casualties. Instead of federal restraint and economy, Lincoln's party

---

[6] Leonard D. White, *The Jacksonians* (New York: Macmillan Co., 1954), p. 141.

promoted active government. Some sixty years of relative Republican dominance began with a reorganization of government designed to implement the Republicans' central political principle of development: more settled land, more industry, more immigration, more urban centers, more commerce. National debt, national taxation and national banks provided a foundation for an energetic national government. The rise in public expenditures during the war and the necessary introduction of new kinds of taxes had changed the "opinion dikes" so as to make national policies possible.[7] Reforms were made in Congress to accommodate the change.

In 1865, the old House Committee on Ways and Means was split in two, with a new appropriations committee receiving appropriations or supply bills and Ways and Means retaining responsibility for revenue bills. The Senate followed suit. Congressional reformers argued that this division of labor would be conducive to economy. The job was too big for a single committee. Specialized committees would be more effective and would increase Congress's ability to direct the activities of government.[8] The consequences were contrary to expectations, as later developments revealed.

The desire for economy was real enough. Relief was desired from the burdens of war—among them, high taxes. Moreover, the earlier system of specificity in appropriations had proved to be inadequate since Congress had to pass supplemental appropriations every session to cover the deficiencies incurred by loosely supervised administrative agencies. The system had collapsed when the foundation for the intended keystone, executive discretion in transferring funds, was undermined by loose administrative practices. Instead of supervising the administrative departments, Presidents had run to Congress for supplementary appropriations. But under Democratic policies of limited federal action, the problem was more an administrative nuisance than a serious political issue. Since the aim was how to govern by spending as little as possible, any spending excesses beyond the appropriated levels involved inconsequential amounts.

In the new environment, however, the question of how to survive while spending more was of great national importance, and congressional procedures for controlling spending were crucial. But complications occurred as a result of separating revenue and appropriations. The subsequent dispersal of responsibility for appropriations bills

---

[7] V. O. Key, Jr., *Parties, Politics, and Pressure Groups*, 5th ed. (New York: Thomas Y. Crowell and Sons, 1964), pp. 222-27.

[8] Woodrow Wilson, *Congressional Government* (Boston: Houghton-Mifflin Co., 1913), p. 152.

to the legislative committees which began a decade later, was un-stoppable. The attempt of the House Appropriations Committee to block popular legislation was the cause. In retribution, Congress stripped the committee of its centralized control over funding. A look at the kinds of appropriations bills first stripped away is illuminating: agriculture, forestry, and rivers and harbors legislation—all politically important and expensive, particularly rivers and harbors. By now congressmen had discovered the many advantages of the "pork-barrel." A rise in expenditures was one consequence of the dispersal.

A shift in revenue policy made the separation of functions and the scattering of appropriations endure. Protective tariffs had become the Republican party's winning political issue. Not only were tariffs now the main source of government revenues but also, of course, they served to encourage the development of domestic manufacturing. In fact, the production of revenue was an incidental result of tariff policy. The levels of tariff deemed desirable to protect industry generated seemingly inexhaustible surpluses. Revenues no longer governed expenditures and revenue policy was subordinate to the wider goals of encouraging commercial enterprise.

The impulse for increased spending existed, the conditions for increased spending existed—and spending increased. There was no institutional check in Congress to control it. Strains or inequities caused by protective tariff measures were not felt fully due to compensatory programs. General tax reform eased the immediate burden and federal budget surpluses were available to fund new programs. Shrewd use of appropriations measures proved politically and fiscally expedient. Proliferation of government-financed pensions was one program, but even it paled beside the internal improvement programs that followed.

A centralized appropriations committee turned into a battery of "little legislatures," each enjoying a monopoly over both legislative and appropriations measures in particular substantive areas. As a final measure, congressional leaders staffed the appropriations committee with members satisfied to play a limited role. "Thus it came about that instead of one road into the Treasury—and that a thorny one—there were seven or eight primrose paths and 'as many byroads as there were members of these appropriations committees'." [9]

A fiscal crazy quilt existed 20 years later as the pressures for spending worked upon a fragmented appropriations process imbedded

[9] Lucius Wilmerding, *Control of Spending* (Reprint of 1943 ed., Hamden, Conn.: Shoe String Press, 1970), p. 141.

in legislative committees. Congress abetted the forces that mocked the process. The economy theme, ignored in practice, received its due in the hypocritical procedure whereby appropriations were deliberately underestimated for the sake of the appearance of reduced spending. Deficiency appropriations were then passed to supplement funds available to the various agencies. To further dilute responsibility, regular appropriations bills were considered and passed under the guidance of the legislative committees while special supplemental and deficiency bills were routed through the appropriations committees.

The original vision of responsible controls on the exercise of the power of the purse was fully obscured. Concern for executive tyranny was replaced by concern for executive weakness. The power of the President and the Treasury Department was sapped: The President knew less than Congress about expenditure amounts, had little control over the kinds of spending, and was kept from the deliberations that shaped spending measures. The Treasury Department served as little more than a recorder of estimates. For a time it was even forbidden to revise estimates and was restricted to pointing out discrepancies between spending and revenue—with no power to reconcile the differences.

Near the end of the 19th century, with executive leadership precluded and congressional leadership dispersed, the "reign of the speakers" began. The leadership gap was filled with elective party leaders. Majority rule literally became Congress's mode of action for 20 years as the various speakers of the House of Representatives ruled through the special powers vested in their office, primarily control over the Rules Committee.[10] The weight of the office coupled with the kind of party support a speaker could marshal through judicious exercise of his powers, brought Congress to its highest peak of control over national affairs. Concentrated power orchestrated by the speaker moved Congress in truly unprecedented ways.

Political dissatisfaction leading to the "rebellion" and overthrow of "Czar Cannon" in 1910 arose out of the uses of the speaker's power, not the possession of power per se. The Progressive movement desired a thorough reform because it disliked the policies followed by Speaker Cannon. Other political forces worked at reform as a means to improve the existing arrangements.

---

[10] Speaker Reed by an artful interpretation of the House rules gained a command post in Congress. Secure in his stronghold, he enticed supporters with prospects of committee assignments. From control over rules, speakers conquered committees until their writ ran throughout Congress.

One issue adding to general public dissatisfaction with Congress under the speakers' rule was the continuing crisis over appropriations. The schedule for passing appropriations had grown shorter, and shorter, until scarcely more than a few months were allowed to receive, review, and approve appropriations measures. Deficiency requests increased, while chaos in the executive agencies made a mockery of Congress's exercise of the power of the purse. There was no effective control over the use of funds. In passing the Sundry Civil Appropriations Act of 1909, Congress assigned the President the task of publicizing imbalances in revenue and expenditures and of recommending measures for reconciling the differences.[11] But it gave him no power except persuasion to accomplish his task should he recommend either budget cuts or tax increases.

The fervor of the language used by the Progressives to describe the circumstances in Congress strikes some responsive chords today. Congress does not educate, debate, or lead the nation, it was argued. It passes conglomerate laws in which no two schemes pull together. "If there is a coincidence of principle between several bills of the same session, it is generally accidental; and the confusion of policy which prevents intelligent cooperation also, of course, prevents intelligent differences and divisions. . . .It has no common mind, and if it had, has not the machinery for changing it."[12] When the "rule of the speakers" ended, a decentralized Congress was without means to exercise its power. It accepted recommendations to reform the appropriations process since there was no alternative.

A generation of criticism and political maneuver preceded the reform in the appropriations process contained in the Budget and Accounting Act of 1921. The reform was not an isolated incident. Rather it was hammered out during the era of Woodrow Wilson's "New Freedoms" as part of a package of reforms whose fundamental purpose was to establish effective national leadership acting in full public view. Moreover, it was required in view of the change in the nation's revenue structure. Internal taxes had replaced tariffs as the major revenue source and this shift exposed the operations of the federal government to direct scrutiny in the same way state and local governments had always been exposed. Thus, the first congressional report to recommend a national budget system, issued by the Good committee in 1912, rested its case on the ground that a unified budget system would yield comprehensive and responsible control of fiscal

---

[11] Joseph P. Harris, *Congressional Control of Administration* (Washington: The Brookings Institution, 1964), pp. 56-58.

[12] Wilson, *Congressional Government*, p. 325.

policy.[13] Executive supervision over the expenditure of funds would enhance congressional control.

The Executive appropriations process. Federal budget reform is never a simple organizational matter, independent of political effects. The new system created in 1921 cast the mold for the present appropriations process, and subsequently changed the relationship between Congress and President.

The Budget and Accounting Act of 1921 vested the power to reconcile spending and revenue estimates in the executive. The Bureau of the Budget was created within the Department of the Treasury as a supervisory agency to prepare the budget, since Congress was reluctant to entrust such powers directly to the President. The President was authorized to recommend to the Congress a coordinated plan for fiscal policy and to justify overall financial action with the assistance of the Bureau of the Budget.

Within the Congress, as counterweights to the new powers of the executive, a single appropriations committee was reconstituted in each house. These unified committees were expected to restrain spending by treating the amounts requested by the executive as appropriations ceilings. Another congressional counterweight to the Bureau of the Budget, the General Accounting Office (GAO) was set up to provide Congress with information about actual spending.

When Congress changed the budget process, its intention was to promote congressional control over spending. Greater centralization within the executive branch was thought necessary if the executive was to prepare a coordinated budget. Events outside Congress and a shift in public opinion in favor of the presidency left the intent of Congress unfulfilled. The enormous rise in federal spending that has occurred in the last 50 years was unimagined when the present budget process was created, as was the concentrated energy that the executive branch developed. And the administrative implications of the reform act were not understood. The President's responsibility to initiate budget proposals proved a power sufficient to elevate the executive branch to a position of authority in fiscal policy.

The goal was to find and implement an effective fiscal system, one that coordinated budgeting and accounting functions and provided for democratic control. But a good system is hard to find. The National budget process framed in the 1921 act had two requirements, centralized executive control and improved congressional supervision.

---

[13] *The Need for a National Budget System,* House Document No. 854, 62nd Congress, 2nd session (1912).

The executive gained more control over budget policy through centralized management, but Congress became specialized and fragmented. As a result, the expectation for a shared exercise of financial powers went aglimmering. In its place, an Executive budget process emerged.

Changes made after 1932 further improved the management capabilities of the President. Recommendations contained in the "Brownlow report" (1936) and the report of the Senate Select Committee (1937), along with several executive orders on the Bureau of the Budget (1939, 1940), all moved in the same direction: to coordinate the executive's management tools. Command over financial matters was given to the Bureau of the Budget, and the President was made its commander-in-chief.

Gradually, tighter coordination and control of the executive agencies involved in financial matters brought overall fiscal policy fully under executive scrutiny. The premise underlying such measures was that the President better than the Congress could provide effective leadership over fiscal policy. Two recent examples show how durable the premise is. The first Hoover Commission recommended (1949) transfer of the GAO's accounting duties to the Treasury Department, and the second recommended (1955) further Bureau of the Budget controls through changes in budget accounting methods.

As it worked out, the Budget and Accounting Act gave Congress few of the benefits it anticipated. A narrow criterion for measuring the effect of the 1921 act is whether Congress knows what is actually spent. Information about actual spending is necessary in order to control spending. The creation of the GAO was a monument to the Congress's realization that it had not known what was being spent. And there had been no compelling political reason for it to care. Protective tariffs had raised abundant revenues. Loose appropriations had given government agencies easy access to federal monies, and inadequate accounting had obscured backlogs of unexpended funds in agency accounts. While expenditure committees to investigate the uses of funds had always existed as part of the appropriations process, they were little used. As long as appropriations were made and drafts against the Treasury submitted under some plausible interpretation of a statute, Congress had accepted the results. Inadequate investigation by the expenditure committees and simple accounting problems had left Congress ignorant of actual expenditures, of procedures actually followed, and of application of the law.[14]

---

[14] John S. Saloma, III, *The Responsible Use of Power* (Washington: American Enterprise Institute, 1965), pp. 116-19.

The GAO, as originally created and used, turned out to be a "pseudosolution," because initially Congress failed to use it to gain information about agency spending. Subsequent laws, however, have improved its audit and investigative functions and widened the audience for its reports. No longer is it likely to be mistaken for a part of the executive branch.[15]

Congress has made two major attempts, in the reorganization acts of 1946 and 1970, to improve congressional control over budget policies. Neither has accomplished as much as was written into the legislation. Practical problems diluted the effects of some changes and others were not fully implemented.

The reorganization act of 1946, the more sweeping of the two, contains the outlines of most reform proposals heard today. It was designed to duplicate in Congress the deliberations on the budget that occur in the executive branch. For example, it called for a "legislative budget" wherein Congress would establish an expenditure ceiling, calculated from budget requests as modified by revenue projections, to govern the budget total finally adopted. Responsibility for drawing up this legislative budget was to be given to a Joint Committee on the Budget. The practical difficulties of agreeing on such a budget proved so great that this provision was finally repealed in the reorganization act of 1970.

Other provisions addressed the committee system. In an effort to make Congress more efficient, its internal structure was simplified and the number of standing committees reduced. The latter, however, led to a proliferation in the number of subcommittees. Second, a major effort was made to reduce jurisdictional conflicts among committees through a redefinition of committee tasks. However, the creation of rules governing committee jurisdiction buttressed the power of committee chairmen—an unanticipated support for the seniority system—and therefore tended to make committees more independent of one another. These reforms were supposed to facilitate a new congressional role, legislative oversight. The effect was to strengthen the influence of the internal organization of Congress on substantive actions while weakening the party leadership structure through which Congress has compensated for the effects of formal structures.

---

[15] Statement by Frank H. Weitzel, Acting Comptroller General in U.S. Congress, Joint Committee on the Organization of Congress, *Organization of Congress*, 89th Congress, 1st session, part nine (Washington: U.S. Government Printing Office, 1965), pp. 1363-95.

A different approach to improving the control of Congress over financial action was taken in 1970.[16] The attempt was more modest—to provide Congress with better information. The 1970 reorganization act requires five-year projections of program costs, supplementary budget messages in mid-year, hearings by the appropriations committees on the overall budget, and presentation of executive justifications for budget requests.

The models of congressional action implicit in the reorganization acts of 1946 and 1970 are similar, with some interesting differences. Both attempts tried to arm Congress with information and procedures that would permit it to duplicate the executive's actions on the budget. Both accepted the concept of single, specialized committees on appropriations and attempted to refine the division of labor already in existence. Both reforms resulted in endorsements for the basic features of the appropriations process. Both reforms selected the appropriations committees to bear the brunt of the task of assessing the appropriations proposals of the executive. Thus, the 1946 and 1970 reforms treat the appropriations committees as only one of many committees, each with a particular task to perform. The job of the appropriations committees, however, is to exercise a unique congressional power. The rules and organization of Congress explicitly recognize the special task of appropriations, but congressional practice condones program funding by jealous legislative committees (see Table 25).

The differences between the two reform attempts are significant. While the 1946 effort tried to superimpose a centralized power upon the appropriations and revenue committees in order to coordinate spending and revenue measures, the 1970 act merely called for more information and more supervision by the appropriations committees. The practical problems experienced in trying to implement the broader features of the 1946 act counselled the more modest effort of 1970.

But the real lessons of the 1946 attempt were not followed in 1970. The basic problem lies in the current type of appropriations process, which is centered in specialized appropriations committees, but which depends on separate actions to propose, fund and finance programs that are nowhere combined. As long as these conditions exist, nothing can be done to restore congressional control over the power of the purse.

A second major problem is the near impossible schedule confronting the appropriations committees; study, hearings, and report

---

16 U.S. Congress, House, Committee on Rules, *Legislative Reorganization Act of 1970*, 91st Congress, 2nd session, House Report 91-1215.

Table 25

BUDGET AUTHORITY, FISCAL YEARS 1970-73

($ billions)

	1970 (Actual)		1971 (Actual)		1972 (Estimate)		1973 (Estimate)	
	$	%	$	%	$	%	$	%
Trust Funds	62.3	27.4	68.4	26.8	77.4	28.4	85.0	27.3
Permanent Budget Authority	21.9	9.6	22.9	8.9	24.1	8.8	26.0	8.3
"Backdoor" Authority a	7.4	3.2	14.8	5.8	2.1	.8	20.6	6.6
Nondiscretionary Budget Authority b	91.6	40.2	106.1	41.5	103.6	38.0	131.6	42.2
Total Budget Authority c	227.0	—	254.7	—	272.7	—	311.0	—

a Excludes trust funds and permanent budget authority portions of backdoor authority.

b Figures are rounded.

c Excludes all offsetting receipts.

Source: Office of Management and Budget.

must be completed within five months if the resort to continuing measures is to be avoided. The practical problems alone are sufficient to raise doubts about the present system.

The effects of separating appropriations from legislation show up in several different types of congressional "dodges," as well as in some practices within the executive branch. Table 25 reviews the means used by Congress to grant budget authority over the past four years. The shrunken role played by the appropriations committees is measured by the difference between budget authority available to the executive and the amount subject to annual review within the appropriations process. The process established by Congress to provide discretionary review of budget authority is circumvented almost as much as it is used. So-called backdoor financing of programs, making spending authority available by devices other than appropriations, is only one indication of the use of practices at odds with existing rules and procedures.

The question of total spending is beyond the appropriations committees' jurisdiction, as is the more important question of the total results of congressional authorizations. And that is the root of the present dilemma: the appropriations committees, whose members know best the amount and nature of expenditures, cannot exercise control at the beginning or the end of the process. They cannot control the impulse to spend nor can they effectively refine the consequences of the impulse. The legislative committees are in a similar situation. Appropriations committees can only provide the means to implement the decisions of the legislative committees (if ratified by Congress). The experience of the appropriations committees with agency workings cannot be brought to bear fully on assessments of the effectiveness or wisdom of existing programs. And their commitments to certain agencies and programs cannot easily be questioned.

The contrast between congressional and executive procedures for deciding budget policy is best illustrated in the existence of the Office of Management and Budget (OMB, formerly the Bureau of the Budget) within the White House organization and the absence of any similar body within Congress. Financial decisions by the executive are centralized. Budget decisions by Congress are dispersed, first between the two houses and then within each house. In practice, the formal separation of revenue, appropriations and legislative committees sanctions a public irresponsibility. In practice, the special powers of Congress with respect to financial policy are parcelled out among committees. This fragmentation weakens the institution of Congress. Reforms that demand financial information either from the committees or for their use as a means to coordinate financial and legislative proposals are only partly effective. They are little more than exhortation and hardly a substitute for action.

Congress's problem is the absence of any procedure that brings together the legislative, revenue, and appropriations dimensions of policy questions. The executive branch's advantage is the existence of just such a procedure. Congress can learn a lesson from the executive. If it does not, it will have betrayed its obligations and played false its own interests.

Summary

The clash between Congress and President over control of spending can be resolved by reform. Each can claim a "mandate" for its own position in the "battle of the budget."

If Congress is to rise to the present challenge it must construct a new model of the appropriations process, for the models it has known so far are inadequate to the present tasks. The earliest type, the Congressional model, suited a Congress determined to spend little. The second, the National model, was appropriate to a Congress determined to spend funds amply provided by revenue policies, but careless about the effects of its expenditure decisions. The existing type, the Executive model, fits a Congress that has become subservient and responsive to a President who makes the major decisions about the budget.

For 40 years Congress has been judged in popular opinion by the support it provides the chief executive. Its unique power with respect to financial questions has been organized in such a way it can support the President or obstruct him, but seldom can it act on its own. As a result, its prestige is now lower than that of the "do nothing" Congress made famous in President Harry Truman's reelection campaign.

Foremost among the goals of reform is an improvement in the capacity of Congress to confront the full range of budget questions. Laws delegating powers to the President with respect to financial and fiscal policies which successive Congresses have passed provide a conflicting heritage. Congress expects the President both to lead it in formulating general policy and to follow it in executing specific programs. Both overall policy and particular programs now present different types of choices that Congress is ill-prepared to make because of its appropriations process.

6
PROSPECTS FOR A CONGRESSIONAL BUDGET PROCESS

Since everyone has an interest in the budget process, reconciling the conflicting interests is the major obstacle to budget reform. Changing the key processes through which the government makes decisions on spending will have important impacts on a multitude of federal programs, on national priorities, and on overall fiscal policy.

Specific Proposals for Reform

This chapter briefly summarizes ten proposals for reforming the congressional budget process. The legacy of the past—delegated powers to the President and reduced power for the appropriations committees—hampers congressional initiatives to control budget policy. Taken together, the ten recommendations that follow could substantially strengthen the appropriations process as Congress's major management tool.

- consolidate and simplify the budget,
- reorganize the appropriations committees along program lines,
- revise the congressional calendar,
- enhance the role of the *Economic Report of the President,*
- limit annual authorization of programs,
- use a special bill for appropriations increases,
- reduce "backdoor" financing,
- use a budget "scoreboard,"
- improve expenditure analysis,
- create an Office of Program Analysis and Evaluation.

Consolidate and simplify the budget. If Congress is to regain an important role in the direction of budget policy, the complexity of the budget presented to Congress must be reduced. The use of a government-wide program budget—as recommended in the AEI report on the fiscal 1973 budget—would help to focus attention on the key choices to be made and the changing priorities that would result. Another vital change is to consolidate the existing 13 appropriations bills into a smaller number of major program categories to facilitate coordinated review and evaluation.

One scholar has proposed that the separate measures should be consolidated into five general bills:[1] (1) agricultural and natural resources—to include the Departments of Agriculture and Interior, and public works; (2) general government—to include most of the independent offices along with the judiciary, the legislature, and the Executive Office of the President; (3) human resources—to include the Departments of Housing and Urban Development, Labor, and Health, Education and Welfare, along with the Veterans Administration, and District of Columbia; (4) national security—to include the Departments of Defense and State, United States Information Agency, foreign aid and military construction; (5) science and technology—to include the Departments of Commerce and Transportation, National Aeronautics and Space Administration, National Science Foundation, and the Smithsonian Institution. This proposed arrangement, which parallels the pattern of consolidation followed in OMB when it reviews requests, reflects the major functions now carried out by the federal government.

Consolidating programs would have several advantages. The appropriations committees could more effectively consider the various programs presented to them in the budget if these programs were grouped together by functional category. Moreover, by this arrangement (and any arrangement is debatable) the members of Congress and the public could better understand, discuss and make choices about the spending priorities of the budget.[2] Such consolidation appears even more necessary in the light of the cabinet-level reorganization recently undertaken by the President.

Another approach to budget simplification is to achieve national goals by decentralized means. Two such policies are revenue sharing, both general and special, and tax credits. These policies would free

---

[1] Stephen Horn, *Unused Power: The Work of the Senate Committee on Appropriations* (Washington: The Brookings Institution, 1970), pp. 226-29, 264-73.

[2] See William Proxmire, Part I, in *Congress and the Budget* (Washington: American Enterprise Institute, forthcoming).

Congress from the need to calculate the detailed implications of measures intended to accomplish very complicated policies on the local level. They would also free Congress from the maze of hundreds of particular and conflicting programs that balloon the budget into encyclopedia size. Revenue sharing is a strategy that extends federal funds for general or special purposes and retains a role for the federal government, but does not require elaborate decisions of Congress or the executive branch about detailed and circumstantial expenditures. Tax credits, as shown in Chapter 3, are another means that permits the national government to pursue policy ends without encumbering Congress or the executive in detailed review and supervision over expenditure measures.

When too many demands are placed upon our budget authorities, their ability to make effective choices is reduced. Techniques that lessen the range and type of calculations required of federal officials would be a partial and practical remedy.

Reorganize the appropriations committees. The relative unity possessed by the executive branch accounts for much of its effectiveness. The Congress could improve its deliberations on the budget and strengthen its hand vis-à-vis the executive by reorganizing the subcommittee structure of the appropriations committees along program lines. Comprehensive program review is complicated by preserving a subcommittee structure in the appropriations committees which is patterned after department and agency lines that have been or are in the process of being abandoned. The executive's perspective depends upon a consolidated review and management of administrative programs. A unified perspective could yield useful information and improve Congress's response to executive initiatives.

If the existing subcommittee structures of the appropriations committees cannot be changed, the benefits of committee consolidation could be achieved by revamping the operations of these committees as follows: Combined subcommittee hearings would be held on the consolidated appropriations bills after the general committee hearings. These combined hearings would proceed with the examination of the requests and presentations by agency officials just as the separate subcommittees do now. Next, the markup sessions could occur within the existing subcommittees with one difference—namely, that combined subcommittee sessions and markup sessions would be held in order to resolve differences and coordinate proposed bills.

Perhaps more basic is the need to strengthen the role of the House Appropriations Committee vis-à-vis its individual subcommittees. At the present time, the parent committee performs little review and exercises only modest control over the deliberations of its components. A center within the committees could be created to resist the centrifugal subcommittee practices if the power of the committee chairmen were strengthened. If each of the various suggestions for strengthening the overall power of the committee are adopted, it would become even more important to make the subcommittees more responsive to the will and broader outlook of the full committee and thus of the Congress itself.

Revise the congressional calendar. Congress begins its appropriations work with the receipt of the President's budget in late January and ideally should complete it by the beginning of the new fiscal year, July 1. Resort to temporary "continuing" appropriations—which permit government operations to continue pending the delayed appropriation—has increased as Congress has struggled with the task of considering ever larger numbers of more complicated appropriations bills within a six-month period. In the past 10 years, 45 existing appropriations measures have been extended into new fiscal years through continuing resolutions.[3] Proposals to correct this problem focus on one of two possibilities, shifting the fiscal year to a calendar-year basis or resorting to separate fiscal and legislative sessions.

An alternative proposal, less disruptive and more effective, would begin the congressional budget process with the fiscal year. For more than 100 years Congress has followed a schedule that compels it to inquire about, to deliberate, and to decide budgetary questions within six months. The job just cannot be done, certainly not effectively, within this schedule. The executive spends more time preparing its proposals than Congress does in responding to those proposals. Fortunately, there is no compelling reason why Congress needs to limit itself in this way, why it should not begin its budgetary process six months earlier than it does at present.

A congressional budget process that began with the fiscal year could use the six months leading up to the submission of the President's budget to examine the foundations for the detailed proposals to come. As part of this examination, public hearings probing into the economic condition of the nation could be held. An outline of the economic constraints and program objectives that are expected to frame the next year's budget could be roughed out in Congress

---

[3] Data derived from U.S. Senate, Committee on Government Operations, *Financial Management in the Federal Government*, 92nd Congress, 1st session (Washington: U.S. Government Printing Office, 1971), p. 12.

before the budget is received. To conform with the new calendar, the Employment Act of 1946 could be amended to direct the President to submit his economic report in July instead of January.[4]

In addition, Congress needs to arm itself with a broader perspective on overall public policy. Paralleling the hearings on the state of the nation's economy, the legislative committees could be inquiring into the program objectives and accomplishments of the various agencies. The usual hearings held by these committees as part of their oversight function should be coordinated with budget issues. Budget policy and spending priorities could be integrated in policy positions developed by party leaders. Program authorizations should be completed by the legislative committees before the appropriations committee begins its work. The great responsibilities now placed on the shoulders of the appropriations committee could be more equitably distributed, greater participation by other congressional bodies gained, and more information elicited.

From January on, the appropriations process could proceed much as it does now. But a calendar revision as outlined above could provide information within the Congress to give more meaning to the choices presented in the budget. It would, in essence, give Congress a running start on the prodigious task of budget review.

Enhance the role of the Economic Report of the President. In the Employment Act of 1946, the Congress established the Joint Economic Committee, which some academic observers have called the "most exciting contemporary innovation of Congress." This is the congressional committee that takes the widest view of the budget's economic and fiscal policy aims. The *Economic Report of the President* is the document that provides the broadest discussion of the budget's underpinnings and its impact. Congress's interest in economic policies and its own role in the budget process merge in the hearings on the economic report held by the Joint Economic Committee.

The significance of the report is now muted because the President's Budget Message and State of the Union address are customarily delivered to the Congress at about the same time (except for 1973 when the President substituted a series of State of the Union messages). As a result, Congress has little opportunity to study the President's economic report before the budget rush begins. A chance to influence public opinion is also lost. If the report were submitted

---

[4] Ernest Griffith, Joint Committee on the Organization of Congress, *Organization of Congress*, 89th Congress, 1st session (Washington: U.S. Government Printing Office, 1965), part 5, pp. 811-21.

and discussed at the beginning of the fiscal year, Congress could begin its own preparations for appropriations hearings at the same time the executive does. A variety of perspectives on economic policy could be set forth and debated within Congress. The enlarged perspective on the budget gained through hearings in Congress on appropriate fiscal objectives could be an important step forward.

Limit annual authorizations of programs. With the 1946 reorganization act, Congress took on the function of legislative oversight and this function has led to the greatly increased use of annual authorizations. Before 1946, Congress normally concurred in the President's request for relatively permanent authorizations. (Some type of authorizing legislation for an activity must be on the books before Congress can appropriate money for it.) Any discussion of restoring control over the budget must reckon with the question of annual authorizations.

Annual authorizations complicate—some say, overtax—the appropriations process by requiring two different sets of committees, legislative and appropriations, to consider the same object in turn. One result is a certain amount of delay in the passage of appropriations bills and these delays have been occurring more frequently as the portion of the budget requiring annual authorization has increased. Yet it is questionable that an end to annual authorizations would greatly affect the log jam. Recent delays are caused primarily by the need to reconcile differences between the House and Senate versions of appropriations bills. And these differences are generated primarily in the complexity and significance of the programs themselves.

In many instances, annual authorization by the legislative committees has become part of the legislative oversight function. The process involves regular review of program goals, procedures and costs—which takes time but yields benefits in the form of greater participation, useful information and more focused inquiry. Yet, a modification of present practices is needed. First, Congress should revise its procedures to require completion of annual authorizations before the budget is submitted by the President. In this way, the potential conflict between legislative and appropriations committees would be reduced and delay lessened. Second, the authorization committees should not prescribe dollar floors or ceilings on the programs whose authorization or reauthorization they are recommending. Deciding precise magnitudes of government programs should be the province of the appropriations committees. Decisions about spending for individual programs by appropriations committees could be guided by the constraints accepted by Congress. Initial recommendations about adjustments in program spending would fall to the appropriations committees. (The concept of a special appropriations bill is discussed below.)

Use a special appropriations bill to control spending. Congress's most recent use of a spending ceiling was the Revenue and Expenditure Act of 1968. The act was important because it linked revenue action to establishing a ceiling on outlays, albeit with some exceptions. The major weakness in proposals for expenditure ceilings is the limited extent to which Congress adheres to them in making individual expenditure decisions.

An alternative way of controlling total spending levels is for Congress to use a spending ceiling coupled with a special appropriations bill. A spending ceiling resolution, setting either a target or a mandatory limit, could be applied either to budget authority or budget outlays. However it is defined, the spending ceiling should set forth the upper limit for proposed total spending.

The change (up or down) in the spending level proposed for the new fiscal year would be presented in a special appropriations bill—a fourteenth appropriations bill, or a sixth bill if consolidated appropriations bills were used.[5] It could be sponsored by the chairmen of the appropriations committees. Besides strengthening the direction of the whole committee over adjustments in total spending, the special bill would clearly identify the increase (or decrease) in congressional spending both in total and in particular program areas.

Under this arrangement, subcommittees of the appropriations committees would be limited to the amount of funds appropriated in last year's bill for the activities under their purview. Increases in this year's appropriations bills by the subcommittees would be permitted only to compensate for inflation. So last year's appropriation's bill adjusted by a standard inflation factor, such as 3 percent, would be the spending ceiling for new appropriations by each subcommittee. Within the limits, subcommittees could increase, decrease, or eliminate program spending as they preferred.

Changes in overall spending levels proposed for the new fiscal year—either the usual increase or, on occasion, a reduction—would be made in the special appropriations bill. Thus, the piecemeal approach to granting budget authority would be corrected. Current

---

[5] The proposal was suggested in conversations with Professors William A. Niskanen and Aaron Wildavsky of the Graduate School of Public Policy Research, University of California, Berkeley.

appropriations bills would limit proposed new spending levels, adjusted for inflation. Within these limits, each appropriations subcommittee would be free to reallocate funds among different programs within its jurisdiction as it saw fit. A special appropriations bill would include increases (or decreases) in total funding. Committee chairmen would supervise the special appropriations bill as befits their responsibility to oversee appropriations. In this way specialization could occur in subcommittee operations and coordination could occur in whole committee decisions.

Reduce backdoor financing. During the House debate on the spending ceiling bill in 1972, a direct solution to the expenditure problem was proposed: strict enforcement of the rules to prevent circumvention of the appropriations process. Congress would move toward reestablishing control over the budget if it were to enforce strictly a revised Rule XXI of the House of Representatives.[6] That rule protects the jurisdiction of the appropriations committee against other committees reporting out appropriation measures. The major exception to the jurisdiction of the appropriations committees is the custom of giving the House Ways and Means Committee control of several programs that involve large expenditures—social security, revenue sharing, and some public assistance. The principal devices Congress uses to authorize expenditures by government agencies without an appropriation are public debt transactions, note cancellations, revolving funds, and contract authority.

Backdoor spending is attractive because it is expedient. It offers an easy way to fund programs that, for various reasons, might not fare well in the normal appropriations process. It is permitted even though it is contrary to the established appropriations process. Its use disperses control over the power of the purse. Table 26 shows the use of backdoor spending over the past four fiscal years.

If Congress desires to improve its powers and increase its political effectiveness it must redeem its own commitments to a single appropriations process. Scrutiny by the Rules Committee to check legislative proposals that permit backdoor funding would improve the situation. Amending Rule XXI would prevent further erosion of the appropriations process and once again place expenditure decisions in the proper perspective—that is, all expenditure decisions placed together and measured against revenue calculations.

---

[6] See testimony of Representative Thomas M. Pelly, Joint Committee on the Organization of Congress, *Organization of Congress*, 89th Congress, 1st session, (Washington: U.S. Government Printing Office, 1965), pp. 1569-95.

Table 26
BACKDOOR FUNDING
(fiscal years 1970-1973)

	Total Budget Authority [a]	Backdoor Authority [b]
1970		
$ Millions	227,000	14,600
Percent of total	100	6.5
1971		
$ Millions	254,700	21,800
Percent of total	100	8.6
1972		
$ Millions	272,700	10,200
Percent of total	100	3.7
1973		
$ Millions	311,000	28,700
Percent of total	100	9.2

[a] Total budget authority, excluding all offsetting receipts, is the sum of current and permanent authorizations.
[b] Includes trust funds and federal funds.
Source: Data supplied by Office of Management and Budget, Office of the Director.

Use a budget scorecard.[7] Much of the current discussion about improving congressional consideration of the budget stresses the need to relate actions on individual appropriations to the budget totals. Omnibus appropriation bills and expenditure ceilings are two approaches often suggested. In fact, both have been tried, the omnibus bill in the early 1950s and the expenditure ceiling in the late 1940s, but have not endured.

A much more modest proposal, by no means an ultimate solution, is the device of a "budget scorecard" that would show the cumulative effect of individual budget decisions on the overall state of federal finances. Essentially this device would enable every congressional committee reviewing a given item to treat that item as the marginal case during its review. But the scorecard would merely be an informational aid. Its use would not alter the existing organization or procedures used by the Congress to act on individual bills. Rather, the scorecard would be a handy analytical mechanism to guide the

---

[7] For an earlier version, see Murray L. Weidenbaum, *Federal Budgeting: The Choice of Government Programs* (Washington: American Enterprise Institute, 1964), pp. 76-81.

existing committees as they followed existing appropriation procedures.

Table 27 illustrates a hypothetical budget scorecard, drawn up on the following two assumptions: (1) that revisions from the original presidential estimates are supplied by some congressional committee or staff (a point to which we will return), and (2) that the estimated deficit for the budget year (in this case 1974) has already been increased by congressional action on previous items (the scorecard of course would work just as well in opposite cases). The information set forth in Table 27 would show the congressional committee acting on the proposed appropriation for aircraft procurement that (1) less revenue is available than was originally projected, (2) earlier congressional actions have enlarged the prospective deficit by increasing expenditures, (3) this item, if enacted at the currently recommended level, would raise the budget deficit for 1974 still further, and finally (4) the surplus predicted by the administration for the following year probably will not occur. The scorecard could be used to tally actions on a variety of expenditure authorizations, appropriations bills, and revenue bills. It could apply to all expenditure authorizations larger than a specified amount, for example, $500,000.

Whether the presentation of such data would change the decisions of individual committees or individual members of the Congress is unknown. It would, however, provide a simple mechanism for members interested in the impact of each individual action on the total budget outcome. It would record the ebb and flow of the current status of the budget picture for the ensuing fiscal year. If Congress was enacting higher levels of spending and thus larger deficits (or the reverse) than the President had proposed, this would be revealed during and not after the end of the budget process.

The scorecard approach itself is politically neutral. Advocates of a larger public sector could use it to help bring about greater spending and at a quicker rate, and vice versa.

Use of the scorecards would require expert staff to record and develop estimates of the expenditure or revenue impact of changes in proposed new appropriations or in revenue bills. (The term appropriations is here used in its broadest sense, actions which permit government agencies to obligate the government to make expenditures. Technically, contract authorizations and authorizations to expend from public debt receipts are also included.) The task of maintaining the scorecard could be assigned to the appropriations committees of each chamber or alternatively, to a new joint committee on the budget, should the Congress decide to establish one. Another possi-

Table 27
HYPOTHETICAL BUDGET SCORECARD

	1973 (Current Year)		1974 (Budget Year)		1975 (Following Year)	
	Presidential submission	Current estimate	Presidential submission	Current estimate	Presidential submission	Current estimate
Unified Budget Totals: ($ billions)						
Receipts	225	228	256	254	290	282
Outlays	250	255	269	272	288	294
Surplus (+) Deficit (−)	−25	−27	−13	−18	+2	−12
Item Under Consideration: ($ millions)						
Appropriation for Air Force Procurement of Missiles						
Amount being considered:						
Expenditures	1,452	1,552	1,582	1,682	1,680	1,780
(Appropriations)	(1,670)	(1,670)	(1,573)	(1,773)	(1,770)	(1,880)

Note: Increased deficit will require higher taxes or larger public debt.

bility would be to build on the Scorekeeping Report now issued by the Joint Committee on Reduction of Federal Expenditures. Alternatively, the capabilities of the General Accounting Office might be expanded.

Improve expenditure analysis. Lack of information and professional management studies weaken Congress's consideration of the budget. It is not a lack of information so much as the absence of critical evaluations of the programs and activities scattered across the federal landscape that seems to trouble Congress. A disturbing potential for mistakes lurks in appropriations decisions because the right kind of information is not available at the right time.

What is needed, especially by congressmen who are not members of the appropriations committees, are evaluative studies of the effectiveness and costs of alternate approaches to given objectives. The provision in the reorganization act of 1946 that the GAO provide "expenditure analysis" is empty because of inaction by Congress.[8] Congress could activate this provision, asking GAO to prepare evaluations of agency actions and to concentrate on selected program areas of interest and importance.

In addition, the GAO could render valuable assistance to the appropriations committees if Congress were to authorize it to review the budget justifications that the individual agencies submit to the Congress. The data contained in these justifications, critically evaluated by GAO prior to the appropriations hearings, could arm Congress in the manner that the Budget and Accounting Act of 1921 intended.

Create an Office of Program Analysis and Evaluation. The 1968 and 1972 efforts to put a ceiling on expenditures broke down on the question of what programs to reduce. The information required to make comparative judgments about where to adjust spending was not available. This is one reason why Congress resorted to the formula of percentage cuts with selected exemptions in 1968.

Wilbur Mills, chairman of the Ways and Means Committee in the House, and others have proposed the creation of an independent agency to evaluate existing programs.[9] Congress needs some way to assess the comparative costs and benefits of federal programs and to evaluate alternative approaches. The idea is not new. For example,

---

[8] A balanced review of the controversy is in John S. Saloma, III, *Congress and the New Politics* (Boston: Little, Brown and Company, 1969), pp. 145-53.

[9] *A Proposed Approach to the Spending Problem*, Legislative Analysis No. 11 (Washington: American Enterprise Institute, 1967).

106

Senator Homer Ferguson proposed, in 1952, to create a Legislative Bureau of Audit and Efficiency as a new approach to economy and control. Although the Bureau of the Budget was expected to provide this kind of information for Congress, it has focused on meeting the requirements of the President.[10]

The essential ingredient in any attempt to control expenditures is critical evaluation of federal programs. Congress set itself to the task of legislative oversight with the 1946 reorganization act. If oversight is to be effectively pursued, Congress needs professional assistance beyond that provided by its existing staff and executive sources. This assistance could be provided by the creation of an Office of Program Analysis and Evaluation empowered to provide analytical studies of program costs, benefits and suggested alternatives. Evaluative research is now a virtual monopoly of the executive branch, to the extent it is used at all. As imperfect as it may be, it is generally better than the kind of information on which Congress must now rely when it inquires about the effectiveness of programs. An Office of Program Analysis, located within the GAO, would be autonomous and nonpartisan. Gaining the full benefit of program evaluation requires congressional acceptance of critical results. Congress must realize, as Presidents have found with presidential commissions, that the results may be unexpected.

The Purpose of Reform

For the past 40 years Congress has cooperated in sustaining what has been described in this analysis as an executive budget process. It has done so on the basis of two assumptions: we can always spend more and we are generally in substantial agreement about what is most important. Whatever the validity of these assumptions in past years, the President is challenging their validity for today, and this challenge has disrupted the basis of the working relationship between Congress and the executive branch.

The appropriations process must become the central feature of congressional action. Legislation by means of appropriations is the keystone for the greatest political work: "the regulation of various and interfering interests."

With reform, Congress can become an independent, equal and active partner in the budget process. Without reform it will remain a secondary political body. And that would indeed become a crisis.

---

[10] U.S. Senate, Committee on Government Operations, *Financial Management in the Federal Government*, 87th Congress, 1st session (Washington: U.S. Government Printing Office, 1961).

APPENDIX A

Congressional Action on the
Fiscal 1973 Budget

Current public discussion of congressional and presidential roles in the federal budget process has produced much controversy but a dearth of factual analysis. One of the few positive contributions is buried in a relatively obscure staff report of the Joint Committee on the Reduction of Federal Expenditures. This report presents data not otherwise readily available on congressional actions with respect to the fiscal 1973 budget. Perhaps the most interesting part of the report deals with the expenditure programs that were not contained in the original budget estimates for fiscal 1973 but were added to that budget by the Congress.

Table A-1 identifies and aggregates the estimated expenditure effect of measures that were initiated by the Congress. These measures added $4.4 billion to the original budget estimate of expenditures for fiscal 1973. Where estimates are available, these add-ons are projected over a five-year period, and this figure comes to $29.7 billion. The amounts shown are prior to presidential veto or impoundment.

Table A-1
ESTIMATED COST OF PROGRAMS ADDED TO THE BUDGET BY CONGRESS IN FISCAL YEAR 1973
(\$ in thousands)

Program	Outlays in 1973	Five-Year Cost
General		
Establish congressional Office of Goals and Priorities Analysis	4,500	13,500
Capitol security	3,000	3,000
Service contract wage rates	10,000	250,000
Establish Office of Technology Assessment	2,500	N.A.
Department of Agriculture		
Rural development	470,000	1,700,000
Cooperative forest programs	5,000	92,000
Accelerated reforestation	65,000	375,000
Sawtooth Recreation Area	46,093	46,093
School lunch	200,000	N.A.
Youth Conservation Corps	30,000	90,000

Table A-1 (*Continued*)

Program	Outlays in 1973	Five-Year Cost
Department of Commerce		
Sales of U.S. passenger vessels	12,600	12,800
Marine mammal protection	3,700	17,800
Tuna development	1,000	3,000
Jellyfish control	—	1,600
Commercial fisheries development	1,500	26,400
Federal elections campaign	2,000	10,000
Coastal zone management	12,000	186,000
Spokane Expo-74	11,500	11,500
Economic development	607,500	3,177,500
Department of Defense		
POW and MIA leave accumulation	13,400	13,400
Dam inspection	5,000	45,000
Rivers, harbors and flood control	592,922	836,966
Department of Health, Education, and Welfare		
Black lung benefits	968,712	4,000,000
Higher education	N.A.	16,000,000
Impacted area school aid—Postal Service	8,500	17,000
Food for the elderly	100,000	250,000
National Institute of Aging	20,000	Open-end
Sickle Cell Act	25,000	115,000
Cooley's anemia control	3,700	8,175
Drug listing	2,000	10,000
Department of Interior		
Buffalo National River	8,367	27,877
Oregon Dunes Recreation Area	15,200	15,200
Gunboat "Cairo"	2,261	3,200
Metallurgy research center	6,000	6,000
Mining and minerals research	25,200	222,000
San Francisco Wildlife Reservation	20,300	20,300
Tinicum Marsh preservation	2,250	2,250
Gulf Island Seashore extension	3,337	3,565
Longfellow Historic Site	204	1,480
Fossil Butte National Monument	4,847	5,005
Thaddeus Kosciuszko Home	139	592
Sitka National Monument	174	1,184
Puukohola Heiau Historic Site	1,041	1,041
Hohokam Pima National Monument	152	2,555
Piscataway Park addition	1,525	1,525
Reclamation projects	256,651	256,651
Reclamation feasibility studies	3,625	3,625
Seal Beach Wildlife Refuge	40	525
Glen Canyon Recreation Area	37,500	37,500
Cumberland Island National Seashore	11,986	32,194
Grant-Kohrs Ranch Historic Site	2,150	2,585
Perry's Victory Memorial	5,547	5,547
Delaware Watergap	31,400	65,000
St. Croix Wild River	2,550	7,275

Table A-1 (*Continued*)

Program	Outlays in 1973	Five-Year Cost
Department of Justice		
Deputy U.S. Marshals—pay increase	2,129	11,883
Department of Labor		
Longshoremen's and Harbor Workers Compensation Amendments	5,300	15,000
Department of State		
Salmon Fishery Act	N.A.	2,000
Department of Transportation		
Motor vehicle information	23,000	108,000
Towing vessel operator licensing	375	1,575
Airport and airways development	N.A.	700,000
Emergency rail facilities restoration	N.A.	58,000
Veterans Administration		
Assistance to medical schools	50,000	170,000
Paraplegic housing grants	3,500	26,000
National cemeteries	23,100	217,500
Other Independent Agencies		
Civil Service—firemen's retirement	6,700	33,500
District of Columbia—Eisenhower Convention Center	14,000	14,000
Equal Employment Opportunity Agencies— Continued Equal Employment Opportunity Commission—enforcement	15,900	106,762
Railroad retirement—20% increase	298,000	N.A.
Railroad retirement benefit increase	68,000	N.A.
Small Business Administration—disaster loan interest rate reduction	50,000	N.A.
Small Business Administration—minority business	160,000	163,500
National Commission on Consumer Finance—extension	500	500
Total	4,390,410	29,664,630

Source: Joint Committee on Reduction of Federal Expenditures, *1973 Budget Scorekeeping Report,* Staff Report No. 9 (Washington: U.S. Government Printing Office, 1972), Table 6.

APPENDIX B

Types of Budget Authority

Neither Congress nor the President can gain effective control over total budget authority as it now is. A large portion of total budget authority in any fiscal year is authorized in such a way that some appropriations are exempted from discretionary review by anyone. Federal monies appropriated by trust fund legislation are "uncontrollable." Permanent appropriations are "uncontrollable" since outlays are contingent upon outside events beyond the control of Congress. And "backdoor" appropriations permit agencies to obligate Treasury receipts without requesting appropriations from Congress.

Table A-2 presents the amount of budget authority available during each of the past four fiscal years, broken down by type of appropriations action required of Congress.

Table A-2
BUDGET AUTHORITY[a]
1970-1973
($ in billions)

Description	1970 Actual	1971 Actual	1972 Estimate	1973 Estimate
Current budget authority				
Appropriations				
Federal funds	135.3	148.4	169.2	179.3
Trust funds[b]	c	0.8	1.7	0.1
Backdoor authority				
Federal funds	5.4	14.3	0.3	19.7
Trust funds	0.8	5.7	—	1.7
Total current authority	141.6	169.2	171.2	200.8
Federal funds	(140.7)	(162.7)	(169.5)	(199.0)
Trust funds	(0.9)	(6.5)	(1.7)	(1.8)
Permanent budget authority				
Appropriations				
Federal funds	21.9	22.9	24.1	26.0
Trust funds	55.2	60.6	67.6	76.8
Backdoor authority				
Federal funds	2.0	0.5	1.8	1.0
Trust funds	6.3	1.3	8.1	6.4

Table A-2 (*Continued*)

Description	1970 Actual	1971 Actual	1972 Estimate	1973 Estimate
Total permanent authority	85.4	85.3	101.6	110.2
Federal funds	(23.9)	(23.4)	(25.9)	(27.0)
Trust funds	(61.5)	(61.9)	(75.7)	(83.2)
Total budget authority	227.0	254.7	272.7	311.0
Federal funds	(164.6)	(186.3)	(195.3)	(226.0)
Trust funds	(62.3)	(68.4)	(77.4)	(85.0)
Total backdoor authority included above	(14.6)	(21.8)	(10.2)	(28.7)
Federal funds	(7.4)	(14.8)	(2.1)	(20.6)
Trust funds	(7.2)	(7.0)	(8.1)	(8.1)

[a] Excludes all offsetting receipts.
[b] Includes authorizations for increases in employment taxes.
[c] Less than $50 million.
Source: Office of Management and Budget, Office of the Director.

114

1973 PUBLICATIONS TO DATE

U.S. BALANCE OF PAYMENTS POLICY AND THE INTERNATIONAL MONE-TARY SYSTEM, Gottfried Haberler (18 pages, no charge)

REVIEW—1972 SESSION OF THE CONGRESS AND INDEX OF AEI PUBLICA-TIONS (51 pages, $2.00)

NEW INITIATIVES IN NATIONAL WAGE AND PRICE POLICY, Murray L. Weidenbaum (5 pages, no charge)

THE WILLIAMS-JAVITS PENSION REFORM PROPOSAL (57 pages, $2.00)

ELECTIONS IN SOUTH VIETNAM, Howard R. Penniman (246 pages, cloth $7.50, paper $3.50)

PROPOSED ALTERNATIVES TO TAX-EXEMPT STATE AND LOCAL BONDS (48 pages, $2.00)

SOME OBSERVATIONS ON JAPANESE-AMERICAN ECONOMIC RELATIONS, Gottfried Haberler (15 pages, no charge)

THE BURKE-HARTKE FOREIGN TRADE AND INVESTMENT PROPOSAL (39 pages, $2.00)

U.S. IMPORT QUOTAS: COSTS AND CONSEQUENCES, Ilse Mintz (85 pages, $3.00)

PUBLIC HOUSING: AN ECONOMIC EVALUATION, Richard F. Muth (61 pages, 3.00)

INCREASING THE SUPPLY OF MEDICAL PERSONNEL, Charles T. Stewart, Jr. and Corazon M. Siddayao (81 pages, $3.00)

SELECTED 1972 BOOKS AND STUDIES

Domestic Affairs

AIRPORTS AND CONGESTION: A PROBLEM OF MISPLACED SUBSIDIES, Ross D. Eckert (71 pages, $3.00)

NIXON, McGOVERN AND THE FEDERAL BUDGET, David J. Ott, Lawrence J. Korb, Thomas Gale Moore, Attiat F. Ott, Rudolph G. Penner and Thomas Vasquez (61 pages, $2.50)

VALUE ADDED TAX: TWO VIEWS, Charles E. McLure, Jr. and Norman B. Ture (97 pages, $3.00)

FREIGHT TRANSPORTATION REGULATION: SURFACE FREIGHT AND THE INTERSTATE COMMERCE COMMISSION, Thomas Gale Moore (98 pages, $3.00)

SIGNIFICANT DECISIONS OF THE SUPREME COURT, 1971-72 TERM, Bruce Fein (65 pages, $2.00)

THE MODERN CORPORATION AND SOCIAL RESPONSIBILITY, Henry G. Manne and Henry C. Wallich (107 pages, $5.75)

EMPLOYMENT POLICY AT THE CROSSROADS: AN INTERIM LOOK AT PRESSURES TO BE RESISTED, William Fellner (28 pages, $2.00)

International Affairs

DEFENSE IMPLICATIONS OF INTERNATIONAL INDETERMINACY, Robert J. Pranger (31 pages, $2.00)

THE FLOATING CANADIAN DOLLAR, Paul Wonnacott (95 pages, $3.00)

TROUBLED ALLIANCE: TURKISH-AMERICAN PROBLEMS IN HISTORICAL PERSPECTIVE, 1945-1971, George S. Harris (263 pages, cloth $8.50, paper $4.50)

INTERNATIONAL MONETARY PROBLEMS, Conference proceedings with papers by Armin Gutowski, Fritz Machlup, and Friedrich Lutz (136 pages, cloth $8.50, paper $4.00)

THE NIXON DOCTRINE, Melvin R. Laird, Robert P. Griffin, Gale W. McGee, and Thomas C. Schelling (79 pages, cloth $5.00, paper $2.50)

INCOMES POLICIES ABROAD, PART II, Eric Schiff (53 pages, $2.00)

Matching Needs and Resources: Reforming the Federal Budget by Murray L. Weidenbaum, Dan Larkins and Philip N. Marcus continues AEI's series of annual reviews of the federal budget. This volume is more wide-ranging than last year's study. It includes, in addition to a review of the programmatic content of the new budget, a discussion of the fiscal policy that the budget proposes. It also examines three topics of intense debate at the present time: first, a proposal for removing the inequities created by the system of personal deductions in the federal income tax; second, an analysis of the effectiveness of wage-price controls during 1972 and the prospects for 1973; and third, the outlook for congressional budget reform and the presentation of a specific set of reform proposals.

Dr. Murray L. Weidenbaum is Edward Mallinckrodt distinguished university professor at Washington University in St. Louis, Missouri, and an adjunct scholar at the American Enterprise Institute for Public Policy Research. Dr. Weidenbaum served as assistant secretary of the treasury for economic policy during 1969-1971 and as a fiscal economist with the Bureau of the Budget from 1949 to 1957. Dr. Dan Larkins is a staff economist with the American Enterprise Institute. Dr. Philip N. Marcus is a research associate in political science at the American Enterprise Institute.

$3.00

 American Enterprise Institute for Public Policy Research
1150 Seventeenth Street, N.W., Washington, D. C. 20036